The New
Wider World

Second Edition COURSEMATE

for **CCEA** GCSE Geography

Peter Richardson

Skills unit developed by
Simon Ross

Contents

Introduction

About this book

This New Wider World Coursemate matches the content of *The New Wider World* to your own GCSE Geography specification, and follows the same order. It is a pocket companion for your course and provides a summary of the core information you will need to know and revise for your GCSE Geography examinations.

CCEA specification

Scheme of assessment and specification structure

The scheme of assessment comprises three assessed components:

Component	Percentage
Assessment Unit 1 (1½ hours)	40%
Assessment Unit 2 (1½ hours)	40%
Fieldwork investigation	20%

The subject content is divided into six themes:

Theme A: Atmosphere and Human Impacts
Theme B: Physical Processes and Challenges
Theme C: Ecosystems and Sustainability
Theme D: Population and Resources
Theme E: Economic Change and Development
Theme F: Settlements and Change

Themes A, B and C are assessed through Assessment Unit 1. Themes D, E and F are assessed through Assessment Unit 2.

Each assessment unit contains three compulsory multi-part questions worth 40 marks each.

Fieldwork investigation

The specification states that the investigation should be based on either a decision making task, a problem solving task or a hypothesis testing task. The following structure should be used in carrying out the investigation:

- Stage 1   Planning
- Stage 2   Data Collection
- Stage 3   Report – Development
- Stage 4   Report – Interpretation, Evaluation and Conclusion

The report based on the fieldwork should not exceed 2,500 words. The use of ICT throughout the investigation is encouraged, e.g.

- word processing of all or part of the report
- using spreadsheets to store data and generate graphs or charts.

How your Coursemate is organised

Your Coursemate follows the same structure and order as the topics in your specification. Most of the information is from *The New Wider World*, so your book acts as a companion to both *The New Wider World* and your own specification. Your Coursemate is organised in the following way:

- The **Unit** and **chapter headings** match those used in the specification.
- The **page references** to *The New Wider World* at the beginning of each chapter tell you which pages in the textbook your Coursemate refers to.
- The **Key ideas** relate to those that appear in your specification, and the content of your Coursemate is organised around these.
- **Key words to know** – these are the key geographical words and terms you need to know and be able to use.
- **Check this!...** – doing these questions will check that you know and understand the key concepts in each chapter.
- **Back to...** is a cross-reference to *The New Wider World* for finding more information. It can also be a cross-reference to other information in your Coursemate.
- **Case studies** are based on the case studies and place studies in *The New Wider World*, and **Case Study Extras** are new case studies written especially for your specification. Where relevant these will: refer you back to the textbook for more information; tell you how to get the best from your case study; provide links to other topics; provide updates to the case study, which may be accessed via a link from the Nelson Thornes website at www.nelsonthornes.com/newwiderworld/ and include questions that encourage you to learn the case study so that you can make appropriate use of it in your examination.
- **Exam practice** – there is a total of 40 marks for questions relating to each theme, spread over three chapters. This reflects the structure of the CCEA examination. You can check your answers by going to *The New Wider World Coursemates* website at www.nelsonthornes.com/newwiderworld.
- Each exam practice question is followed by **exam tips** to provide help and advice on answering the question.

At the end of this book you will find a chapter on **geographical skills**. This gives information on the basic geographical skills you will need for the interpretation, presentation and analysis of geographical information and data throughout your Geography course and in your examinations.

> All references to *The New Wider World* in your Coursemate are to the Second edition.

1

Weather systems and forecasts

1 Weather is made up of different elements which can be measured

Surrounding the Earth is a layer of gases called the **atmosphere**. It is within this atmosphere that our climate and weather processes operate.

Weather is the hour-to-hour, day-to-day state of the atmosphere. It includes **temperature**, sunshine, cloud cover, **precipitation**, atmospheric pressure, wind speed and wind direction. It is short-term and can be localised in relatively small areas. Therefore it is possible to experience several types of weather within one afternoon or when making a short journey.

Climate is the average weather conditions of a place taken over a period of time, often 30 years. It is the expected, rather than the actual, conditions. It is long-term and is often applied to sizeable parts of the globe, e.g. the equatorial and the Mediterranean climates.

Britain has:
- a variable climate, which means that the weather changes from day to day, which makes it difficult to forecast (see pages 6–8)
- a moderate climate, which means that extremes of heat or cold, drought or prolonged rainfall, are rarely experienced.

Elements of the weather

The weather we experience each day is made up of several elements:
- **Temperature** is measured in **degrees Celsius (°C)**. The lowest temperature ever recorded in the world was –89.2°C at Vostok, Antarctica on 21 July 1983 and the highest was 58°C at Al'Aziziyah in Libya, on 13 September 1922.
- **Precipitation** is any form of water (rain, hail, sleet or snow) which falls from the atmosphere to the Earth. Precipitation is measured in millimetres (mm).
- **Wind speed** is a measure of the rate that air moves within the atmosphere. It is usually measured in kilometres per hour (km/h). The highest wind speed recorded is 372 km/h at the top of Mount Washington in the USA in 1934.
- **Wind direction** indicates where the wind is coming from, i.e. the source region. Hence northerly winds hitting Northern Ireland are cold as they have come from the Arctic regions. Wind direction is described using the eight points of the compass.
- **Atmospheric pressure** indicates the pressure that the gases in the atmosphere are exerting on one part of the Earth's surface and is measured in millibars (mb). The highest level of atmospheric pressure ever recorded was 1083 mb (Agata, Siberia in 1968) and the lowest was 870 mb (Philippines, 1979).

Measuring the weather

The professional weather forecasters at the Meteorological (Met) Office use very expensive and sophisticated equipment to measure the

KEY IDEAS

1 Weather is made up of different elements which can be measured.

2 Air masses affect the weather of the British Isles.

3 Variations in weather patterns can be linked to changes in air pressure.

4 Weather forecasts are made by observing the weather.

Key words to know

Atmosphere
Weather
Temperature
Precipitation
Climate
Degrees Celsius (°C)

weather, but it is possible to take adequate measurements using homemade or inexpensive equipment. Figure 1.1 shows the instruments required to measure the five elements of the weather described above.

- The **maximum/minimum thermometer** should be placed in the shade and facing north so that it measures the air temperature rather than the heat of the sun. The alcohol in the tube expands upon heating and pushes the mercury up the tube where the maximum metal indicator will be left to mark the maximum temperature. When the temperature falls the retreating alcohol pulls the mercury up the minimum column where it leaves the minimum metal indicator at the minimum temperature. Both metal indicators can be reset using a magnet. The key to the working of this thermometer is that the alcohol can flow freely past the minimum indicator but the mercury cannot.

- **The rain gauge** should be placed away from buildings as these affect the amount of rain caught in the gauge. The gauge should also protrude 30cm above the surface of the ground to prevent surface water from entering the container.

- The arrow on the **wind vane** will point to the direction from where the wind is coming. This instrument is sometimes placed on the top of buildings, including churches.

- The **anemometer** shown here is a cup anemometer which measures wind speed by the rotation of the cups on the axle.

- The **barometer** measures changes in atmospheric pressure by way of a small corrugated box which has no air inside it (a vacuum).

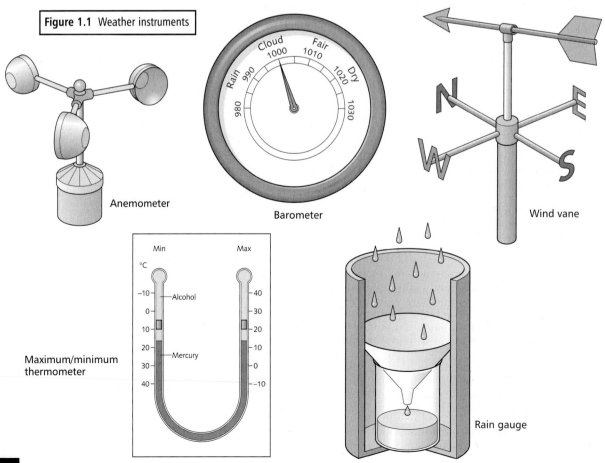

Figure 1.1 Weather instruments

Anemometer

Barometer

Wind vane

Maximum/minimum thermometer

Rain gauge

This small box reacts to changes in atmospheric pressure just as a biscuit tin would to pressure from your hand. As the corrugated box changes shape in response to changes in pressure, the very small movements are magnified by a series of levers to move the hands on the face of the barometer.

Check this!...

1 Explain the difference between weather and climate.

2 Suggest two reasons why a thermometer should not be located on a south-facing wall.

3 Which weather instrument would always give the same reading inside or outside a building?

2 Air masses affect the weather of the British Isles

An **air mass** is a large body of air with uniform characteristics, i.e. temperature or moisture content. An air mass forms when air remains stationary over a place for several days. During this time the air is likely to assume the temperature and humidity properties of that area (Figure 1.2). Britain is affected by four main air masses, though at different times. Air masses are classified according to:

- the **latitude** (distance from the Equator) at which they originate, as this determines their temperature, i.e. giving either cold polar air (**P**) if to the north, or warm, tropical (**T**) air if to the south
- the surface over which they develop, as this affects their humidity and precipitation, i.e. giving either wet maritime air (**m**) if over the sea, or dry continental air (**c**) if over the land.

When these different air masses move towards the British Isles, they bring with them their own characteristic type of weather (Figure 1.2).

Key words to know

Air mass
Latitude

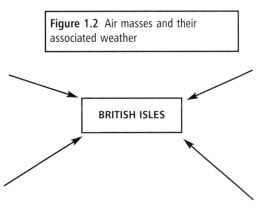

Polar maritime (Pm) air from the north-west
Very common over Britain. Gives cool conditions with heavy showers or longer periods of rain. Good visibility between showers. Winds are often strong to gale force.

Tropical maritime (Tm) air from the south-west
Very common over Britain. Warm (not hot) in summer and mild in winter. Often long periods of steady rain or drizzle with hill fog/low clouds. Poor visibility. Winds are moderate to fresh.

Figure 1.2 Air masses and their associated weather

BRITISH ISLES

Polar continental (Pc) air from the east and north-east
Very cold in winter when it is most likely to occur. Usually gives dry weather. Eastern Britain may get snow (moisture collected from passage over North Sea). If it occurs in summer it gives warm, dry conditions. Fresh winds.

Tropical continental (Tc) air from the south and south-east
Only occurs in summer when it gives very hot (heat-wave) and dry (drought) conditions. Can last several days and often ends with thunderstorms. Gentle winds. Dust affects visibility.

3 Variations in weather patterns can be linked to changes in air pressure

Depressions

It is the meeting of air masses with different characteristics that produces the changeable weather we experience in Britain. For much of the year our climate is dominated by the passage of **depressions** (Figure 1.3).

Key word to know

Depression

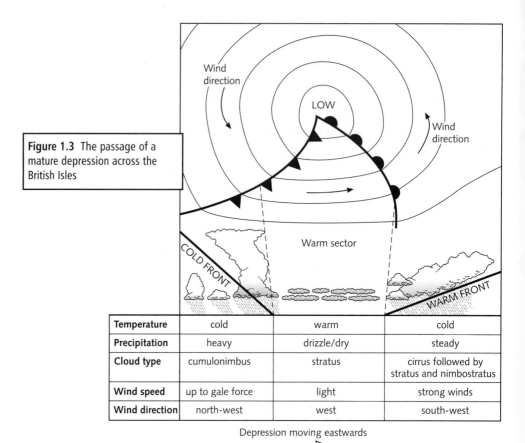

Figure 1.3 The passage of a mature depression across the British Isles

		Warm sector	
Temperature	cold	warm	cold
Precipitation	heavy	drizzle/dry	steady
Cloud type	cumulonimbus	stratus	cirrus followed by stratus and nimbostratus
Wind speed	up to gale force	light	strong winds
Wind direction	north-west	west	south-west

Depression moving eastwards

- A **depression** (**low pressure system**) originates over the Atlantic Ocean when a mass of warm, moist tropical air from the south meets a mass of colder, drier, heavier polar air from the north. The two masses of air do not mix easily due to differences in temperature and density and as a result the lighter, warmer air begins to rise over the denser, colder air in an anticlockwise direction. The boundary between the two air masses is called a **front**.
- As the lighter, warmer air moves towards the denser, colder air, it is forced to rise over the cold air at a warm front. When the denser, colder air moves towards the warm air, it undercuts the warm air, forcing it to rise at a cold front. In both cases the rising warm air is cooled and some of its water vapour content condenses, producing cloud and frontal rain. As the cold front travels faster (65–80 km/h) than the warm front (30–50 km/h), the fronts eventually merge to form an occluded front. This marks the end of the depression because the temperature difference that caused the formation of the depression no longer exists.

Although each depression is unique, the weather they bring to Britain as they travel eastwards tends to have an easily recognisable pattern (see Figure 1.3).

Anticyclones

In Britain **anticyclones** (**high pressure systems**) are experienced far less frequently than depressions but, once established, they can remain stationary for several days and, under extreme conditions, even weeks.

- Their main characteristics are opposite to those of depressions. In an anticyclone, air descends and pressure increases. Winds are very light and blow in a clockwise direction as they move outwards towards areas of low pressure. At times they may even be non-existent and give periods of calm.
- As the air descends it warms and is able to pick up more moisture through evaporation. This usually results in settled conditions with clear skies and a lack of rain (Figure 1.4).

However, there are differences between summer and winter anticyclones.

Summer
- The absence of cloud gives very warm, sunny conditions during the day.
- At night, when clear skies allow some of this heat to escape, temperatures can fall rapidly.
- As air next to the ground cools, condensation can occur and dew and mist may form.
- Thunderstorms are also a risk under 'heat-wave' conditions.

Winter
- Temperatures remain low during the day, due to the sun's low angle in the sky.
- The weather is likely to be dry and bright.
- The rapid loss of heat under the clear evening skies means that nights can be very cold.
- Condensation near to the ground can produce frost and fog which may, due to the sun's lack of heat, persist all day. These conditions can be very dangerous for motorists.

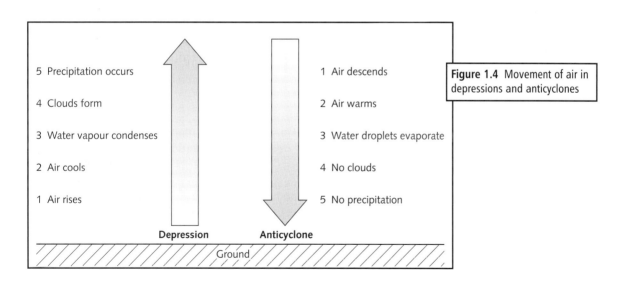

Depression	Anticyclone
5 Precipitation occurs	1 Air descends
4 Clouds form	2 Air warms
3 Water vapour condenses	3 Water droplets evaporate
2 Air cools	4 No clouds
1 Air rises	5 No precipitation

Figure 1.4 Movement of air in depressions and anticyclones

Check this!...

1 Explain how a depression is formed.

2 Match the six pictures in Figure 1.5 on page 6 to the correct weather chart for the weather in Belfast.

3 Describe and explain the weather changes over Belfast shown in Figure 1.5.

4 Why might frost occur during a winter anticyclone?

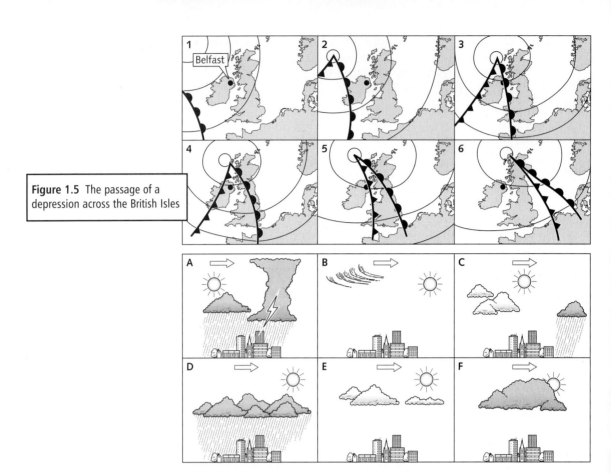

Figure 1.5 The passage of a depression across the British Isles

Key words to know

Relief rainfall
Dew point
Prevailing winds

Back to ...

The New Wider World **p202**
Figure 12.8 which illustrates the formation of relief rainfall.

Check this!...

Why do mountain areas experience relief rainfall?

Influence of relief on rainfall

Relief rainfall occurs when warm, almost saturated air from the sea is blown inland by the wind. Where there is a coastal mountain barrier, the air is forced to rise over it. The rising air cools and, if the dew point is passed, condensation will occur, resulting in cloud formation and precipitation. **Dew point** is the temperature at which the air becomes saturated with water vapour and below which condensation will occur.

Within Northern Ireland the highest annual rainfall average totals (1600 mm) are found in the Sperrin, Antrim and Mourne Mountains.

In the British Isles the **prevailing winds** (dominant wind direction) come from the south-west, collecting moisture as they cross the Atlantic Ocean. They bring heavy rainfall to western parts as they cross the mountains of Ireland, Scotland, Wales and northern England. Eastern areas receive much less rain as they are in the rainshadow area, which is the protected side of a mountain range. Towns like Westport and Bundoran on the west coast of Ireland receive heavy rainfall in late autumn when the sea is at its warmest, and winds blowing over it can pick up most moisture.

4 Weather forecasts are made by observing the weather

Many aspects of our day-to-day lives are influenced by the weather. Therefore it is not surprising that the weather forecast is a source of great interest, especially in the British Isles where the weather is so changeable. The BBC alone broadcasts over 22 hours of forecasts each week.

Range of forecast

A **weather forecast** is a prediction of the type of weather a region will experience over a set period of time. Forecasts are normally given for three time periods:

- short period (for the next 24–48 hours)
- medium range (for the coming week)
- long range (for a month ahead).

In order to forecast the weather it is necessary to observe it and this is done through a network of weather stations across the British Isles as well as on boats and oil rigs. Additional information is available from weather radars (for detecting rainfall), satellites and weather balloons.

Synoptic charts

In order to forecast the weather, it is necessary to observe the present situation – this information can be displayed on a synoptic chart. A **synoptic chart** (Figure 1.6) is a map that uses a range of symbols to show the weather for an area at a specific time. Symbols and numbers are used to show temperature, cloud cover, types of precipitation, wind speed and direction. Pressure is marked on the map using lines called **isobars**. These lines connect places of equal pressure in the same way that contour lines connect places of equal height. If the isobars are close together, wind speed will be high as air rushes from an area of high pressure to an area of low pressure. Conversely, if the isobars are widely spaced winds will be light.

Symbols are used to show the weather conditions at recording stations across the country.

Satellite images

Satellite images (Figure 1.7) are photographs taken from space and sent back to Earth. They are very useful when trying to produce a weather forecast or when predicting short-term changes in the weather. The visible features on satellite images are caused by the reflection of sunlight from clouds or the surface of the Earth. In general, the brighter the cloud the thicker it is.

Key words to know

Weather forecast
Synoptic chart
Isobar
Satellite image

Back to ...

The New Wider World **p206**
Figure 12.17 for information on the use of weather map symbols on synoptic charts.

Back to ...

The New Wider World **p206**
Figures 12.14, 12.15 and 12.16 for a satellite image and synoptic charts of an anticyclone.

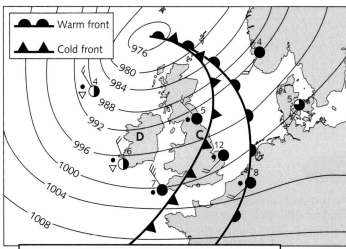

Figure 1.6 A synoptic chart showing a depression over the British Isles on 4 January at 1800 hours

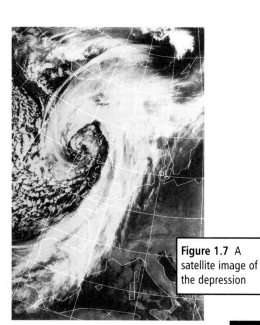

Figure 1.7 A satellite image of the depression

1 Use Figures 1.6 and 1.7 to
help you answer the
following questions.
   a) What is the lowest
      pressure shown on the
      synoptic chart?
   b) Use information from a
      weather station to
      describe the weather
      over south-west Ireland.
   c) Why is there cloud over
      England and eastern
      Scotland?
   d) Which part of the British
      Isles is in the warm
      sector?

2 Explain why the following
   organisations require
   weather forecasts:
   premiership football clubs
   airports
   outdoor pursuits centres.

We receive satellite images from two types of satellite:

- **geostationary satellites** are located over the Equator and take exactly 24 hours to complete one orbit of the Equator
- **polar orbiting satellites** travel from pole to pole at a height of 870 km taking 1 hour 42 minutes to complete an orbit.

A foolproof forecast?

Despite the use of modern computer technology, including satellites, the weather forecasters can get the forecast wrong! A famous example occurred in October 1987 when the weatherman Michael Fish said on a BBC forecast that a lady had rung in to ask if a hurricane was about to hit England. He said no, but the south of England was subsequently battered by a record-breaking storm! This incident is a useful reminder that weather can be unpredictable.

Difficulties in forecasting the weather can be caused by:

- inaccurate observations as a result of human error or equipment failure
- insufficient information from parts of the world, e.g. oceans or remote land areas.

Markets for weather data

The Met Office supplies weather information to a wide range of customers ranging from the media (e.g. television and radio stations) to sporting organisations and the construction industry. The forecasts supplied can help these groups to plan ahead and take action necessary to minimise any negative impacts that the weather may have.

EXAM PRACTICE

1 State which elements of the weather the following instruments measure:
   a barometer
   b anemometer.   (2 marks)

2 Define the term *air mass.*   (2 marks)

3 a With reference to Figure 1.6, identify the weather system located over the British Isles.   (1 mark)

   b Explain why the temperature in the south-east of England is higher than in the rest of the British Isles.   (3 marks)

4 During the summer of 2003 when France was experiencing an anticyclone, 15 000 people (mostly elderly) died. Suggest how a summer anticyclone can cause such a tragedy.   (3 marks)

5 Explain why weather forecasts are important for the farming community.   (3 marks)

Back to ...

The NWW Coursemates website to check your answers to the exam practice question.

EXAM TIPS

If the exam question includes the phrase 'With reference to...', ensure that you refer to the relevant resource(s) in the course of your answer. For a graph quote figures, and for a map use the names of regions or specific features provided on the resource.

2 Climate and its impact

1 The continent of Europe experiences a variety of climates

Figure 2.1 shows the range of climates found across the continent of Europe. Northern Ireland experiences a temperate maritime climate. 'Temperate' means that temperatures are not extreme and 'maritime' indicates that the climate is influenced by being close to the sea.

KEY IDEAS

1 The continent of Europe experiences a variety of climates.

2 Farmers use technology to moderate the impacts of climate.

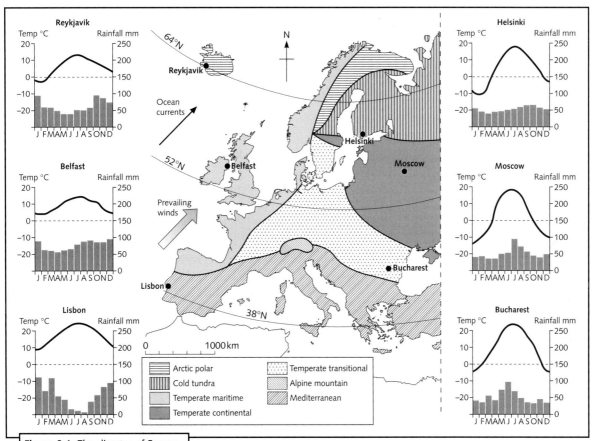

Figure 2.1 The climates of Europe

Factors affecting temperature

Five main factors affect temperature across the continent: latitude, continentality, prevailing winds, ocean currents and altitude.

Latitude (distance from the equator)

Places nearer to the Equator are much warmer than places nearer to the poles (Figure 2.2).

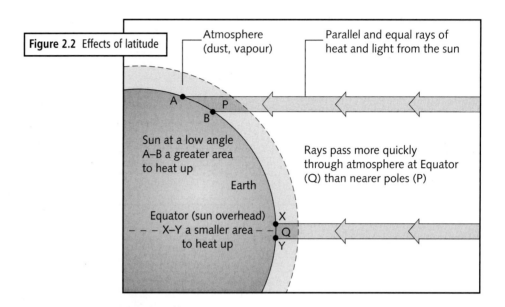

Figure 2.2 Effects of latitude

Back to …

The New Wider World **p201**
Figure 12.3 for a map
showing average July
temperatures in the
British Isles. Notice how the
temperature gets lower the
further north you go.

The New Wider World **p201** Figure
12.4 for a map showing average
January temperatures in the
British Isles. Notice how the
temperature is lower in the east.

At the Equator:
- the sun is always high in the sky, concentrating its heat onto a small area
- the sun's rays have a shorter distance of atmosphere to pass through, so less heat is lost to gases, dust and cloud within the atmosphere.

At the poles:
- the sun is always low in the sky, which means that its heat is spread over a wide area and so temperatures remain lower
- due to the lower angle of the sun, the sun's rays have a longer distance to pass through than places closer to the Equator, resulting in a greater loss of heat.

This is why places to the south of the British Isles can expect to be warmer than places further north.

Continentality (distance from the sea)

- Places that are inland are warmer in summer but colder in winter than places on the coast. This is because the sea takes much longer than the land to heat up over the course of the summer.
- Once warmed, however, the sea retains its heat for much longer, and cools down more slowly than the land during the winter. As Britain is surrounded by sea, it tends to have cool summers and mild winters.
- Despite the fact that temperatures in the Atlantic Ocean are low enough to cause death from hypothermia, it is the largest reservoir of heat in winter, which explains why western parts of the British Isles are warmer than places to the east in winter.

Prevailing winds
- The dominant, or most frequent, winds, known as **prevailing winds**, bring warm weather if they pass over warm surfaces (the land in summer, the sea in winter) and cold weather if they blow across cold surfaces (the land in winter, the sea in summer).
- Prevailing winds in the British Isles come from the south-west and are relatively cool in summer but mild in winter.

Ocean currents
Many coastal areas are affected by ocean currents.
- The North Atlantic Drift is a warm current of water which originates in the Gulf of Mexico. It keeps the west coast of the British Isles much warmer in winter than other places in similar latitudes. Figure 2.3 illustrates this contrast.

Figure 2.3 The influence of ocean currents on temperature

Temperature (°C)	Jan	Feb	Mar	Apr	May	Jun	Jul	Aug	Sep	Oct	Nov	Dec
Belfast (UK): 54°N 6°W	4	4	6	8	11	13	14	14	12	11	7	5
Goose Bay (Canada): 54°N 60°W	−18	−15	−9	−2	−4	11	16	14	10	3	−4	−13

Altitude (height of land above sea-level)
Temperatures decrease, on average, by 1°C for every 100 metres in height. Therefore mountainous areas, e.g. the Mournes and the Sperrins, are generally much colder than lowland areas. The windchill factor makes upland areas even colder, and enables snow to lie for long periods during winter.

Back to …

The New Wider World **p201** Figure 12.5 for a map of the British Isles that shows the effects of altitude on the length of snow cover in winter.

Check this!...
Use Figure 2.1 to answer the following questions.

1 Why does Lisbon experience the highest summer temperatures of the cities shown?

2 Slieve Donard (847 metres above sea-level), is the highest mountain in Northern Ireland. If it is 5°C at Newcastle, which is located at sea-level at the foot of Slieve Donard, what will the temperature be at the summit?

2 Farmers use technology to moderate the impacts of climate
The type of farming practised in any region relates directly to the climate of that area. For example, Northern Ireland with its mild, wet climate is ideal for the growing of grass for cattle, while Mediterranean countries, such as Italy, with their warmer, drier climate, specialise in vines and citrus fruits.

Climatic factors which can influence farming in either positive or negative ways include:
- temperature: most plants will not grow if the temperature drops below 6°C
- the growing season: this is the length of time between the last frost of spring and the first frost of autumn

Back to ...

The New Wider World
pp104–105 for more
information on farming in
southern Italy.

- rainfall: water is essential for plant growth and the greater the average temperature the greater the need for water to sustain plant growth
- wind: high winds can destroy large areas of crops in a short period of time. Winds can also contribute to soil erosion, a problem which is particularly severe in dry climates.

Case Study Extra

Using technology to moderate the impact of climate on farming in Sicily, southern Italy

In the south of Italy (Mezzogiorno), agricultural productivity is heavily reliant on technology to moderate the impact of the drought conditions that result from high pressure weather systems. In Italy 22.8 per cent of the agricultural land is covered by irrigation systems compared with 1 per cent in the UK, but these systems are dependent on a water supply.

The island of Sicily at the southern tip of Italy has a population of 5 million and is heavily reliant on agriculture. Water shortages have been tackled through a number of strategies:

- The government built the Pozzillo reservoir on the island's longest river, the Salso (144 km), to store water for use in the drier months. The dam that created this reservoir was completed in 1964.
- A large group of farmers from the Belice valley formed a consortium to buy an irrigation control system from the high-tech company Motorola in 1994. Water is delivered to the crops through drip or trickle irrigation, which provides a small but frequent supply of water to the plants' roots, thereby reducing water loss. This system ensures that water is not used carelessly, as farmers pay for the quantity they use.

Figure 2.4 Climatic contrasts between Milan (northern Italy) and Palermo (southern Italy)

Milan (45°N 8°E)

	Jan	Feb	Mar	Apr	May	Jun	Jul	Aug	Sep	Oct	Nov	Dec
Temp (°C)	0.3	2.6	6.9	11.2	15.5	19.4	22.4	21.3	18.2	12.7	6.3	1.5
Precip (mm)	51.7	59.7	88.2	125.0	123.6	88.4	64.0	87.7	68.3	83.6	107.0	50.8

Palermo, Sicily (38°N 13°E)

	Jan	Feb	Mar	Apr	May	Jun	Jul	Aug	Sep	Oct	Nov	Dec
Temp (°C)	10.7	10.6	11.4	13.8	17.2	20.9	24.4	24.8	22.6	19.3	15.5	12.3
Precip (mm)	43.9	34.7	30.1	29.4	13.5	8.7	2.3	7.5	27.5	58.6	66.4	68.1

- Rural communities such as San Michele di Gazania, a small settlement of 5000 inhabitants in the east of the island, have been experimenting with the use of recycled water for the irrigation of olive orchards over a 150 ha area.

The future?

In the summer of 2002, 15 000 Sicilian farmers marched on Palermo, the island's administrative centre, to demand action as reservoir levels hit new lows. Climatic change, resulting in drier summers, will mean that further technological advances will be required if farming is to continue in this part of Italy.

Figure 2.5 The island of Sicily

Using your case study

Use this case study to answer questions on how technology can moderate or lessen the impact of climate on farming. You should be able to identify:

- why the climate presents a problem to farmers in this area
- what has been done by the Italian government and the individual farmers to tackle the problem.

Learn it!

1 Which part of Italy is worst affected by drought?

2 What problems does drought bring to the area?

3 How has technology been used to moderate the impact of the climate?

Case Study Extra

Using technology to moderate the impact of climate on farming in County Antrim, Northern Ireland

Horticulture refers to the production of fruit, vegetables and flowers. The horticultural unit in Greenmount Agricultural College in Antrim uses technology to create a 12-month growing season. The climate for Antrim (Figure 2.6) would not permit such an extended season, as much of the produce grown, such as poinsettia and tomato plants, requires temperatures of around 20°C.

The Northern Ireland horticultural sector represents only 4 per cent of Northern Ireland's gross agricultural output (2002), compared with a figure of 15 per cent for this sector in the whole of the UK, but it still makes a significant contribution to the local economy. For example, the market in Northern Ireland for pansies is reported to be worth £2 million alone. Due to the climate in Northern Ireland, many plants have to be grown in greenhouses.

	Jan	Feb	Mar	Apr	May	Jun	Jul	Aug	Sep	Oct	Nov	Dec
Temp (°C)	4.1	4.4	5.6	7.7	10.5	13.4	14.7	14.5	12.5	9.4	6.2	4.7
Precip (mm)	82.8	54.9	58.7	50.5	56.1	65.3	79.1	78.1	82.0	84.9	75.3	83.8

Figure 2.6 Climate figures for Antrim (Aldergrove Airport – average over period 1930–90)

Figure 2.7 A lorry from a local wholesaler picks up a consignment of flowers from the horticultural unit at Greenmount

Technology is used in the greenhouses primarily to create the optimum growing conditions and therefore to maximise yields. A computer system monitors the conditions and makes any necessary adjustments. For example:

- Thermal screens in the roof of the greenhouses can be activated at night to keep heat in, while during the day they can be used to provide shade if required.
- Ventilation systems ensure that heat is distributed evenly around the greenhouse. Heat can be supplied through pipes in the soil or on the benches as required.
- Vents in the roof can be opened to let air circulate. Sensors detect the wind direction and the computer determines which vents are opened.
- Every 1 per cent increase in light gives a 1 per cent increase in productivity. Electric lighting is programmed to allow for optimum photosynthesis or to ensure that

plants flower at the required time.
- Plants can be watered through trickle irrigation. The computer controls the chemical composition of this water to maximise plant growth.

If there is any type of malfunction outside working hours, the computer automatically telephones the member of staff on duty, who is able to access the system via a lap-top computer to make the necessary changes.

Using your case study

Use this case study to answer questions on how technology can moderate or lessen the impact of climate on farming. You should be able to identify how greenhouses and the technology within them can moderate the impact of climate by influencing:

- temperature
- shade
- ventilation
- light
- water.

Learn it!

1 Why it is necessary to use greenhouses to grow tomatoes in Northern Ireland?

2 List three ways in which technology can moderate the impact of climate.

3 How could this type of agriculture benefit Northern Ireland's economy?

EXAM PRACTICE

1 State the meaning of the term *continentality*. (2 marks)

2 Using the information in Figure 2.1, state the highest monthly temperature in Helsinki. (1 mark)

3 Using Figure 2.1, state fully one reason why Lisbon (38°N) experiences a warmer climate than Belfast (54°N). (3 marks)

4 Using Figure 2.1, state fully one reason why Moscow experiences lower temperatures in December than Belfast does. (3 marks)

5 The impact of climate can be moderated through the use of technology. For a named farming area, describe two ways in which technology can moderate the impact of climate on farming. (4 marks)

Back to ...

The NWW Coursemates website to check your answers to the exam practice question.

EXAM TIPS

Where the command 'state fully...' is used, as in questions 3 and 4 above, it is not possible to achieve maximum marks with a one-word answer. For a full answer make sure that you develop all points so that no further clarification is required.

1 Global warming can be caused by human activity

The greenhouse effect

The Earth is warmed during the day by incoming radiation from the sun. The Earth loses heat at night through outgoing infrared radiation. Over a lengthy period of time, because there is a balance between incoming and outgoing radiation, the Earth's temperatures remain constant.

On cloudy nights, temperatures do not drop as low as on clear nights. This is because the clouds act like a blanket and trap some of the heat. Greenhouse gases, which are a natural phenomenon, also act as a blanket, in that they prevent the escape of infrared radiation, just as glass in a greenhouse does. This is known as the **greenhouse effect** (Figure 3.1). Without these greenhouse gases, which include carbon dioxide, the Earth's average temperature would be 33°C lower than it is today (during the Ice Age, temperatures were only 4°C lower than at present).

Greenhouse gases are therefore an essential part of our natural world. However, recent human activity has led to a significant increase in the amount, and type, of greenhouse gases in the atmosphere, e.g. carbon dioxide levels have increased by 25 per cent since the Industrial Revolution. These gases are preventing heat from escaping into space and some scientists, but not all, believe they are responsible for a rise in world temperatures – an issue that is causing global concern. World temperatures rose by 0.6°C during the twentieth century, with seven of the century's warmest years occurring in the 1990s. The process by which world temperatures are rising is known as **global warming**.

KEY IDEAS

1 Global warming can be caused by human activity.

2 Global climate change has both positive and negative impacts.

3 Sustainable solutions to global warming require international co-operation.

Key words to know

Greenhouse effect
Global warming

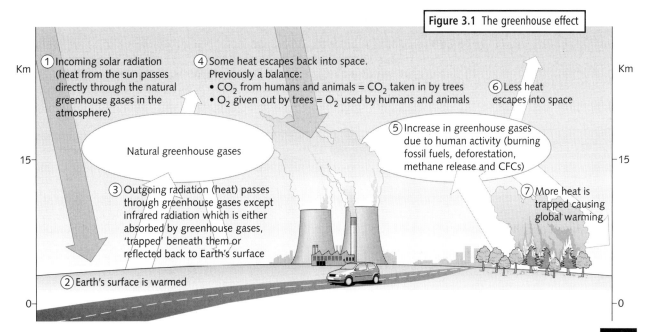

Figure 3.1 The greenhouse effect

① Incoming solar radiation (heat from the sun passes directly through the natural greenhouse gases in the atmosphere)

④ Some heat escapes back into space. Previously a balance:
• CO_2 from humans and animals = CO_2 taken in by trees
• O_2 given out by trees = O_2 used by humans and animals

⑥ Less heat escapes into space

Natural greenhouse gases

⑤ Increase in greenhouse gases due to human activity (burning fossil fuels, deforestation, methane release and CFCs)

③ Outgoing radiation (heat) passes through greenhouse gases except infrared radiation which is either absorbed by greenhouse gases, 'trapped' beneath them or reflected back to Earth's surface

⑦ More heat is trapped causing global warming

② Earth's surface is warmed

Km   Km

Sources of greenhouse gases

- Carbon dioxide is the most important single factor in global warming. It is produced by road vehicles and by burning **fossil fuels** (coal, oil and gas) in power stations, in factories and in the home. Secondary sources of carbon dioxide include deforestation, the burning of the tropical rainforests and the destruction of peatlands.
- CFCs (chlorofluorocarbons) from aerosols, air conditioners, foam packaging and refrigerators are the most damaging of the greenhouse gases.
- Methane is released from decaying organic matter such as peat bogs, swamps, landfill sites, animal dung and farms (e.g. ricefields in South-east Asia).
- Nitrous oxide is emitted from car exhausts, power stations and agricultural fertiliser.

2 Global climate change has both positive and negative impacts

Negative impacts	Positive impacts
• Melting icecaps increase the risk of flooding for some islands and low-lying countries.	• Longer growing season in Europe allowing higher yields (between 1959 and 1993 it increased by 11 days).
• Water expands upon heating, causing rising sea-levels which adds to the threat (Figure 3.3).	• Crops can be grown in northern Europe due to higher temperatures, e.g. maize.
• Areas with sufficient rainfall are likely to get more, resulting in increased flooding (e.g. northern Europe). Regions with insufficient rainfall are likely to get less in terms of both amount and reliability, giving increased drought (e.g. much of Africa).	• Reduction in use of fossil fuels for heating purposes. • Higher rainfall levels in South-east Asia will increase rice yields.
• Ecosystems at all levels may be subject to such a rapid change that plants and wildlife may not have the time in which to adjust.	• Increased yields of wheat in south-east Australia due to higher temperatures. • Presence of a Mediterranean climate in the UK may boost some forms of tourism.
• Crop yields are expected to fall even further in Africa as well as in parts of Asia and Latin America.	• Less snow and ice in the UK would make travelling in winter less hazardous.
• Increased risk from insect-borne diseases, e.g. malaria.	
• Closure of Scottish ski resorts due to lack of snow.	

Figure 3.2 The two sides of global warming

Back to ...

The New Wider World **p220**
Figures 13.23 and 13.24
to identify the impacts of
global warming for the UK
and the world.

Figure 3.3 Jordanstown on the shores of Belfast Lough could be at risk from global warming

Check this!...

1 Why does the rate of global warming appear to be increasing?

2 List the causes of global warming to which you have contributed today.

3 Why are many island nations under threat from global warming?

3 Sustainable solutions to global warming require international co-operation

Key word to know

Sustainable

Kyoto Protocol

Most countries have acknowledged the need to take some form of action to prevent global warming, or at least to slow down the rate at which it is occurring, by reducing their greenhouse gas emissions. A **sustainable** solution is needed – this means protecting the lives of people across the world without creating problems for future generations.

The Kyoto Protocol (a *protocol* is a draft agreement) was devised at a meeting of world leaders in Kyoto, Japan in 1997. If the treaty becomes law, industrialised nations that have signed up to this treaty will be legally bound to reduce worldwide emissions of greenhouse gases by an average of 5.2 per cent below the 1990 levels by 2008–2012.

Opposition to the Kyoto Protocol

- For this treaty to become law, countries accounting for at least 55 per cent of carbon dioxide emissions must be signed up.
- By February 2003 a total of 188 countries had signed up to the agreement but two of the largest producers of greenhouse gases – the USA and the Russian Federation – were still opposed to the Kyoto Protocol and as a result it is yet to become law.
- The President of the USA has defended this stance, stating that the proposals would harm the growth of the American economy.
- The Intergovernmental Panel on Climate Change (IPCC) believes the treaty does not go far enough because gases can remain in the atmosphere for more than 100 years. Emissions would need to be cut by 60 per cent to make a real difference.

Every little helps

Even though international agreement on reducing levels of greenhouse gases may be difficult to achieve, individuals can help to reduce levels of the main greenhouse gas carbon dioxide by making changes in the way they use:

- electricity
- transportation.

Simple changes such as those listed in Figure 3.4 are environmentally friendly and sustainable, and they will also save you money!

Check this!...

1. Why is global warming of interest to world leaders?

2. Explain why the USA opposes the restrictions of the Kyoto Protocol.

3. List three ways in which you could help to slow down global warming.

4. Select three changes from Figure 3.4 which you believe would face the greatest resistance. Give reasons for those changes you have selected.

Use of electricity	Transportation
- Switch off unneeded lights. - Switch off TVs or hi-fis at the mains. (The electricity used in the UK by home entertainment systems while in stand-by mode is the equivalent output of one large power station.) - Buy energy-efficient electrical appliances (A or B ratings). - Avoid leaving the fridge door open for long periods as more energy is then required to keep the fridge at its set temperature. - Dry clothes naturally rather than using a tumble-dryer.	- Buy a fuel-efficient car, - Try to avoid using the car for short journeys. - Join a car pool to go to work or school. - Use public transport, e.g. bus or train. An inter-city electric train causes releases of less than 20 g of carbon dioxide per passenger/km whereas a car emits nearly 40 g.

Figure 3.4 Ways to reduce global warming

EXAM PRACTICE

1 State fully two causes of global warming.

(4 marks)

2 'The benefits of global warming outweigh the problems.' Discuss this statement with reference to places at the global scale.

(9 marks)

Back to ...

The NWW Coursemates website to check your answers to the exam practice question.

EXAM TIPS

The use of the command word 'Discuss' (question 2) indicates that you have to identify those points that would support this statement and any points that would oppose this statement. Weaker candidates will only put forward one side of the debate, so to make sure you maximise your mark put forward both sides.

The New Wider World, pp262–274

4 Crustal movements

1 The surface of the Earth is made up of plates

The lava, ash and other debris emitted by cone-shaped mountains called **volcanoes** and the movement of the earth referred to as **earthquakes** provide dramatic evidence of the power of natural forces. Volcanic activity has taken place in Northern Ireland but it was approximately 60 million years ago! Evidence of this activity can be seen in the landscape: for example, the Giant's Causeway in County Antrim formed as molten lava cooled slowly to create the world-famous hexagonal columns. Another example, also in County Antrim, is Slemish, a small volcanic centre from which lava erupted.

In order to understand the forces behind these events, and more recent volcanic and earthquake activity, it is necessary to examine the structure of the Earth.

If the Earth were the size of an apple, its crust would be no thicker than the apple's skin. Underneath the crust is the mantle where temperatures are so high that rock exists in a semi-molten state. The crust is broken into several large, and other smaller, segments known as

KEY IDEAS

1 The surface of the Earth is made up of plates.

2 Plate boundaries have distinctive characteristics.

3 The ability of a country to plan for and react to an earthquake is closely related to its level of development.

Key words to know

Volcano
Earthquake

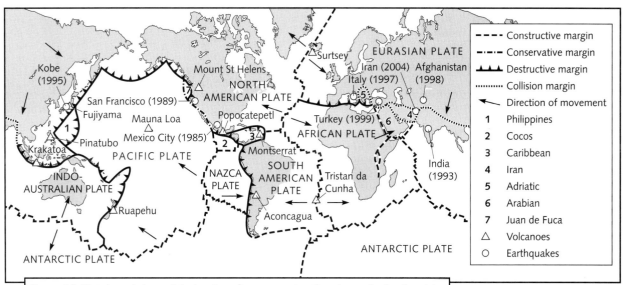

Figure 4.1 Plate boundaries and the location of some recent earthquakes and volcanic activity

Key words to know

Plate
Convection current
Plate movement
Plate boundary
Ring of Fire

◄ **Back to …**

The New Wider World **p263**
Figures 16.3 and 16.5
which show the structure
of the Earth and how
plates move.

Check this!…

1 What is a plate?

2 Why are the plates moving?

3 Why is continental crust permanent?

plates which float, like rafts, on the mantle. Heat from within the Earth creates **convection currents** which causes **plate movement**, perhaps only a few centimetres a year. Plates may move away from, towards, or sideways past neighbouring plates. Plates meet at **plate boundaries** and it is at these boundaries that most of the world's earthquakes and volcanic eruptions occur (Figure 4.1), and where high mountain ranges are located. A belt of volcanoes marks the plate boundaries at the edge of the Pacific plate – this is known as the Pacific **Ring of Fire**. Very little activity takes place in the rigid centre of plates.

Plates consist of two types of crust, continental and oceanic:

- continental crust is older, lighter, cannot sink and is therefore permanent
- oceanic crust is younger and heavier, and it can sink and is constantly being destroyed and replaced.

It is these differences in crust that account for the variation in processes and landforms and the level of activity at plate boundaries (Figure 4.2).

2 Plate boundaries have distinctive characteristics

There are four main types of plate boundary.

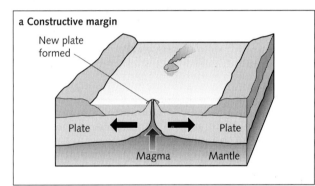

a Constructive margin
New plate formed
Plate ← → Plate
Magma   Mantle

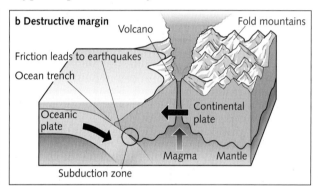

b Destructive margin
Fold mountains
Volcano
Friction leads to earthquakes
Ocean trench
Oceanic plate
Continental plate ←
Magma   Mantle
Subduction zone

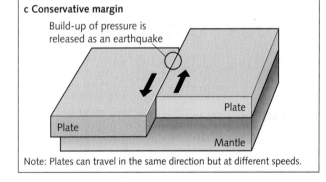

c Conservative margin
Build-up of pressure is released as an earthquake
Plate
Plate
Mantle
Note: Plates can travel in the same direction but at different speeds.

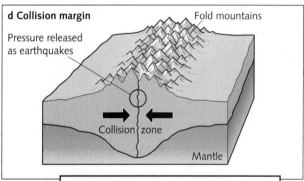

d Collision margin
Fold mountains
Pressure released as earthquakes
Collision zone
Mantle

Figure 4.2 Cross-sections of the plate margins

Constructive margins

- At constructive margins (Figure 4.2a), such as the Mid-Atlantic Ridge, two plates move away from each other.
- Molten rock, or magma, immediately rises to fill any possible gap and forms new oceanic crust.
- The Atlantic Ocean is widening by about 3 cm a year, which means that the Americas are moving away from Europe and Africa.

Destructive margins

Key word to know

Ocean trench

- Destructive margins (Figure 4.2b) occur where plates consisting of oceanic crust move towards plates of continental crust.
- To the west of South America (Figure 4.1), the Nazca Plate (oceanic crust) is moving towards the American Plate (continental crust). Where they meet, the Nazca Plate is forced downwards to form a subduction zone and an associated **ocean trench** (the Peru–Chile trench).
- The increase in pressure as a plate is forced downwards can trigger severe earthquakes.
- As the oceanic crust continues to descend it melts, partly due to heat resulting from friction caused by contact with the American Plate and partly due to the increase in temperature as it re-enters the mantle.
- Some of the newly formed magma, being lighter than the mantle, rises to the surface to form volcanoes (e.g. Cotopaxi) and a long chain of fold mountains (the Andes).

Conservative margins

- Conservative margins are found where two plates slide past one another. As crust is neither being formed nor destroyed at this plate boundary, new landforms are not created and there is no volcanic activity. However, earthquakes can occur if the two plates 'stick' (Figure 4.2c). This is the situation in California, where the San Andreas Fault marks the junction of the Pacific and North American Plates (Figure 4.1).

Back to ...

The New Wider World **pp264–265** for more information on plate margins and **p263** Figure 16.6 for a table showing activity at plate margins.

- A fault is a fracture in the Earth's crust. The American Plate moves more slowly than, and at a slight angle to, the Pacific Plate. Instead of the plates slipping evenly past each other, they tend to stick – like a machine without oil. When sufficient pressure builds up, one plate is jerked forwards sending shockwaves to the surface. These shockwaves caused an earthquake in San Francisco in 1906, when the ground moved by 6 metres, more than 450 people were killed and 28 000 buildings destroyed (Figure 4.1).

Collision margins

- Collision margins are where two plates consisting of continental crust move together. As continental crust can neither sink nor be destroyed, the rocks between them are forced upwards to form fold mountains, e.g. the Himalayas (Figure 4.2d). The Indian Plate is moving into the Eurasian Plate at a rate of 5 cm a year (Figure 4.1).
- This movement, which is still taking place, accounts for major earthquakes such as that which caused the deaths of 13 000 people and left another 600 000 homeless in Gujarat (western India) in 2001.

Check this!...

1 Why is new plate being formed below the Atlantic Ocean?

2 Explain why volcanoes are not found along:
   a) conservative margins
   b) collision margins.

3 Why are the Himalayas getting higher?

Key words to know

Focus
Epicentre
Seismograph
Richter scale

Back to ...

The New Wider World **p270**
Figure 16.25 for more
information on the
Richter scale.

3 The ability of a country to plan for and react to an earthquake is closely related to its level of development

Earthquakes are regarded as a hazard because they can be a threat to people, property and nature. The point at which the earthquake occurs within the Earth's crust is called the **focus**. The **epicentre** is the point on the Earth's surface immediately above the focus of the earthquake.

The shock (or seismic) waves produced by an earthquake can be measured using a **seismograph**. The first seismographs were based on simple tilting mechanisms, but the modern versions are much more sophisticated and capable of recording the smallest tremors.

Seismographs measure the height of the shock waves on the **Richter scale**. It is important to note when using the scale that it is logarithmic, so an increase of one on the scale indicates a ten-fold increase in the magnitude of the earthquake, i.e. an earthquake measuring 5 is ten times more powerful than one measuring 4. The scale is open-ended, ranging from 0 to 8.9, which is the largest magnitude recorded to date (Chile 1960).

Case Study

Kobe, Japan, 1995

Back to...

The New Wider World **pp270–271** for a case study on the earthquake in Kobe, Japan (an MEDC).

Using your case study

Use this case study to answer questions on the impacts of and response to an earthquake in an MEDC. It is important that you can identify short-term and long-term impacts (also referred to as primary and secondary effects) on people and the environment: short-term impacts, e.g. electricity, gas and water supplies were disrupted; long-term impacts, e.g. Hanshin Expressway was closed for over a year.

You may also use information from this case study to contrast the response to an earthquake in an MEDC and an LEDC (Afghanistan).

Update

Go to the *NWW Coursemates* website for a link to the Kobe website giving a detailed report on the impacts of the earthquake and how lessons have been learned from it. Also find the link to the USGS website and look for information on the most recent earthquakes in Japan.

Learn it!

1 Why did this earthquake happen?

2 What factors contributed to the high death toll?

3 What strategies were put in place to prevent this scale of disaster happening again?

Takhar, Afghanistan, 1998

Back to...

The New Wider World **pp272–273** for a case study on the earthquake in Takhar, Afghanistan (an LEDC).

Using your case study

Use this case study to answer questions on the impact of and response to an earthquake in an LEDC. You should identify the short-term and long-term impacts on people and the environment: short-term impacts, e.g. food shortages resulted in thousands of villagers facing starvation; long-term impacts, e.g. Afghanistan does not have the money or technology to improve the quality of buildings or infrastructure

which would help this region cope with any future earthquakes. It is important to note the delay in the response to this earthquake and the reasons for this.

You may also use information from this case study to contrast the response to an earthquake in an LEDC and an MEDC (Japan).

Learn it!

1 Why did this earthquake happen?

2 What factors contributed to the high death toll?

3 Why will Afghanistan struggle to cope with major earthquakes in the future?

Contrasts in responses to earthquakes in an LEDC and an MEDC

The case studies of Kobe in Japan (an MEDC) and Takhar in Afghanistan (an LEDC) demonstrate how a low level of development can greatly undermine the ability of a country to prepare for and respond to an earthquake (Figure 4.3).

Figure 4.3 Predicting and preparing for an earthquake

Prediction	Preparation
It is far harder to predict the time and location of earthquakes than of volcanic eruptions. However, it is possible to: • install sensitive instruments that can measure an increase in earth tremors (seismographs), pressure, and any release of radon gas which would indicate movement in the Earth's crust • map epicentres and frequencies of previous earthquakes to see if there is a location and/or time pattern (this can only give possible timings of an event and not a precise location) • observe unusual animal behaviour – dogs howling, fish jumping, mice fleeing houses (less scientific but has proved useful).	Prediction may only provide at best a few seconds' warning of an earthquake, so it is important that affected areas are well prepared in order to minimise the impacts. Preparation can include: • constructing buildings and roads to withstand earthquakes • training emergency services and having equipment available, e.g. helicopters, ambulances and fire engines • organising emergency services to provide water, food and power • setting up a warning and information system for use on TV and radio (earthquake preparation is part of the Japanese school curriculum).

The effects of earthquakes are usually much greater in LEDCs, e.g. Afghanistan (1998) and Iran (1997 and 2003). Human response to earthquakes is much quicker and more efficient in MEDCs, e.g. the richer countries of Japan (Kobe 1995) and the USA (San Francisco 1989). LEDCs often have to rely upon, and wait for, international aid (Figure 4.4).

Check this!...

1 What evidence is there in Figure 4.4 to suggest that Iran was not prepared for the earthquake?

2 Describe three preparations that earthquake-prone regions can carry out to minimise the impacts of an earthquake.

20,000 killed by Iranian quake

More than 20,000 people were killed at dawn yesterday when an earthquake virtually destroyed the ancient Iranian city of Bam. The quake measured 6.3 on the Richter scale.

The two local hospitals were badly damaged, vastly complicating efforts to treat the injured.

"Seventeen of my relatives are buried under the ruins of my home. They've got to get a move on or all of them will die," said one rescuer, called Ali, as he attempted to shift debris with a spade.

As night fell the streets were packed with frightened survivors, huddling under blankets and hoping that relief supplies would come soon. Ruhollah Bahrami, a shopkeeper, felt let down by the authorities. "If this was the West, we would have had plenty of help by now," he said.

The lack of preparedness and the poverty in a country that experiences dozens of earthquakes a year was all too evident when compared to other earthquake zones. The strength of the earthquake was the same as one that rocked California last week, which damaged one town and killed two people.

Figure 4.4 From *The Daily Telegraph*, 27 December 2003

EXAM PRACTICE

1 State the meaning of the term *volcano*. (2 marks)

2 With reference to Figure 4.1:

  a Identify the type of plate margin located in the middle of the Atlantic. (1 mark)

  b Describe what is happening to the plates that meet at this margin. (2 marks)

  c Explain why these plates are moving in this way. (4 marks)

3 For an earthquake that you have studied, describe:

  a a short-term impact upon people or the environment, and

  b a long-term impact upon people or the environment. (6 marks)

Back to ...

The NWW Coursemates website to check your answers to the exam practice question.

EXAM TIPS

In question 3, focus on the impacts and make sure you know the difference between short-term and long-term impacts of an earthquake. Do not make the mistake of writing down everything you know about your case study.

1 A drainage basin forms part of the hydrological cycle

A **drainage basin**, or river basin, is an area of land drained by a main river and its **tributaries** (streams which drain into larger ones). Its boundary, marked by a ridge of higher land, is called a **watershed**. A watershed, therefore, separates one drainage basin from neighbouring drainage basins. Some basins, like the Mississippi which drains over one-third of the USA, are enormous. At a somewhat smaller scale, Figure 5.1 shows the drainage basins that cover the area of Northern Ireland. All the rivers have their **source**, or origin, in upland areas. The water flows down to the **mouth**, where the water enters a sea or a lake.

Where fresh river water intermixes with saline sea water at the mouth of a river an **estuary** may form, characterised by the presence of mudflats or salt marshes. This part of the river will be affected by the ebb (outward movement of the tide away from land) and flow (inward movement) of the tide. An example within Northern Ireland is the Foyle estuary, which is marked on Figure 5.1.

KEY IDEAS

1 A drainage basin forms part of the hydrological cycle.

2 Processes of erosion, transportation and deposition create the features of a drainage basin.

3 Flood hazards can have physical and human causes.

4 Sustainable river management requires a co-ordinated approach.

Key words to know

Drainage basin
Tributary
Watershed
Source
Mouth
Estuary
Hydrological cycle

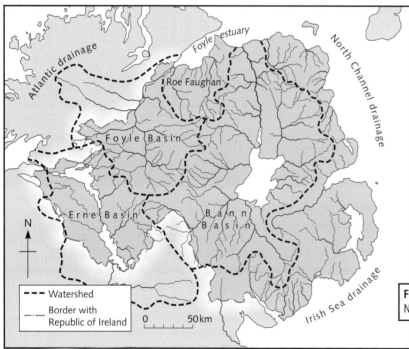

Figure 5.1 Drainage map for Northern Ireland

Drainage basins can store rainwater, either within the river channel itself, or in lakes and in the ground. Excess water is carried back to the sea by rivers. Rivers form part of the **hydrological** (water) **cycle** (Figure 5.2), in which water is constantly recycled between the sea, air and land.

As no water is added to or lost from the hydrological cycle, it is said to be a closed system. A drainage basin forms part of the hydrological cycle but, unlike the hydrological cycle, it is an open system. It is an open system because it has:

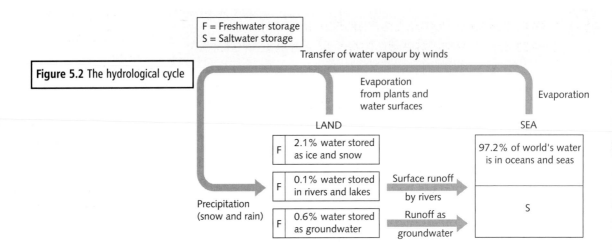

F = Freshwater storage
S = Saltwater storage

Figure 5.2 The hydrological cycle

Transfer of water vapour by winds

Evaporation from plants and water surfaces

Evaporation

LAND

SEA

F | 2.1% water stored as ice and snow

97.2% of world's water is in oceans and seas

F | 0.1% water stored in rivers and lakes

Surface runoff by rivers

S

Precipitation (snow and rain)

F | 0.6% water stored as groundwater

Runoff as groundwater

- **inputs** where water enters the system through precipitation (rain and snow).
- **outputs** where water is lost to the system either by rivers carrying it to the sea or through evapotranspiration. Evapotranspiration is the loss of moisture directly from rivers or lakes (evaporation) or from vegetation (transpiration).

Within the system are stores and transfers (flows):

- **Stores** are places where water is held, e.g. in pools and lakes on the surface or in soil and rocks underground.
- **Transfers** are processes by which water flows, or moves, through the system, e.g. infiltration, surface runoff, throughflow.

Figure 5.3 The drainage basin as an open system

flows | flows | flows

INPUTS | STORES | STORES | OUTPUT

Back to …

The New Wider World **p279** and Figure 17.4 for more detail on the drainage basin system.

Check this!…

1 What term is given to the starting point of a river?

2 What is the watershed?

3 Why is the hydrological cycle referred to as a *closed* system?

Key words to know

Discharge
Irrigation

Back to …

The New Wider World **p280** Figure 17.5 for an example of a hydrograph. A hydrograph is a graph that shows the discharge of a river at a given point over a period of time.

River discharge

- **Discharge** is the velocity of the river times its volume. It is the amount of water in the river passing a given point at a given time, measured in cumecs (cubic metres per second).
- Discharge depends upon the river's velocity and volume.
- Velocity is the speed of the river. It is measured in metres per second.
- Volume is the amount of water in the river system. It is the cross-sectional area of the river's channel, measured in square metres.

Discharge can also be influenced by human activity, e.g. extracting water from the river to water the surrounding land, a process known as **irrigation**, will reduce discharge.

2 Processes of erosion, transportation and deposition create the features of a drainage basin

Energy is needed in any system, not just the drainage basin, for transfers to take place. In the case of a river most of this energy – an estimated 95 per cent under normal conditions – is needed to overcome friction. Most friction occurs at the wetted perimeter, i.e. where the water comes into contact with the river's banks and bed. The channel of a mountain stream, often filled with boulders, creates much friction. As a result, water flows less quickly here than in the lowlands where the channel becomes wider and deeper.

Transportation

Following a period of heavy rain, or below the confluence (where two rivers meet) with a major tributary, the volume of a river will increase. As less water will be in contact with the wetted perimeter, friction will be reduced and the river will increase its velocity. The surplus energy, resulting from the decrease in friction, can now be used for the **transportation** of material. The greater the velocity of a river the greater the amount of material, both in quantity and size, that can be carried. The material that is transported by a river is called its load.

Rivers can transport a tremendous load by four processes:
- **traction** – water rolls stones along the river bed (this requires the most energy)
- **saltation** – particles bounce along the bed in a 'leap-frog' movement
- **suspension** – silt and clay-sized particles are carried within the water flow
- **solution** – some minerals dissolve in the water (this requires the least energy).

Erosion

A river uses the transported material to erode its banks and bed. As the velocity of a river increases, so too does the load it can carry and the rate at which it can erode. There are four processes of **erosion** which all involve the wearing away of the river banks and bed:
- **attrition** – rocks carried by the river collide and break into smaller pieces
- **hydraulic action** – the power of the water dislodges material from the bed and banks
- **corrasion or abrasion** – smaller material rubs against the banks of the river, wearing them away in a sandpapering action
- **corrosion** – weak acids in the water dissolve rocks, e.g. limestone.

Deposition

Deposition occurs when a river lacks enough energy to carry its load. Deposition, beginning with the heaviest material first, can occur following a dry spell when the discharge and velocity of the river drop, or where the current slows down (on the inside of a meander bend or where the river enters the sea).

Key words to know

Transportation
Erosion
Deposition

Back to ...

The New Wider World **p282** Figure 17.11 which illustrates changes in velocity and discharge along the course of a river.

Check this!...

1 Why is the velocity of water expected to be faster in a river's lower course?

2 Why does heavy rainfall lead to higher rates of transportation of the river's load?

3 Which method of erosion can still be effective with a low discharge? Explain your answer.

River features

The processes of erosion, transportation and deposition work together to form features along the course of a river.

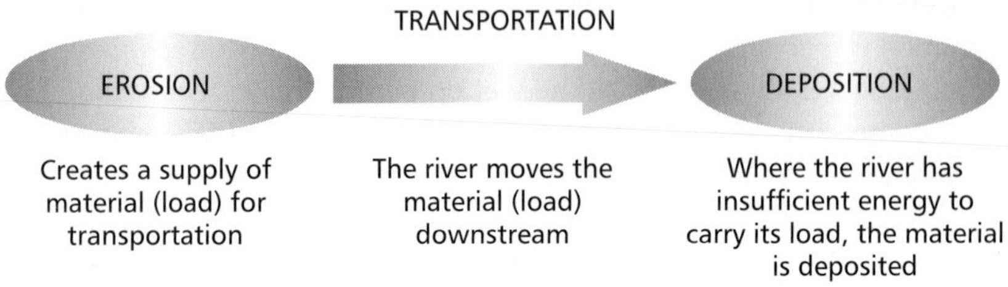

TRANSPORTATION

EROSION → DEPOSITION

Figure 5.4 River processes that shape the land

Creates a supply of material (load) for transportation

The river moves the material (load) downstream

Where the river has insufficient energy to carry its load, the material is deposited

This section focuses on four features found in lowland areas:
- meanders
- floodplains
- levées
- deltas.

Meanders

As a river approaches its mouth it usually flows over flatter land and develops increasingly large bends known as meanders (Figure 5.5). Meanders constantly change their shape and position. When a river reaches a meander most water is directed towards the outside of the bend. This reduces friction and increases the velocity of the river at this point. The river therefore has more energy to transport material in suspension. This material will erode the outside bank by corrasion. The bank will be undercut, collapse and retreat to leave a small river cliff. The river is now eroding through lateral, not vertical, erosion. Meanwhile, as there is less water on the inside of the bend, there is also an increase in friction and a decrease in velocity. As the river loses energy it begins to deposit some of its load. The deposited material builds up to form a gently sloping slip-off slope (Figure 5.5).

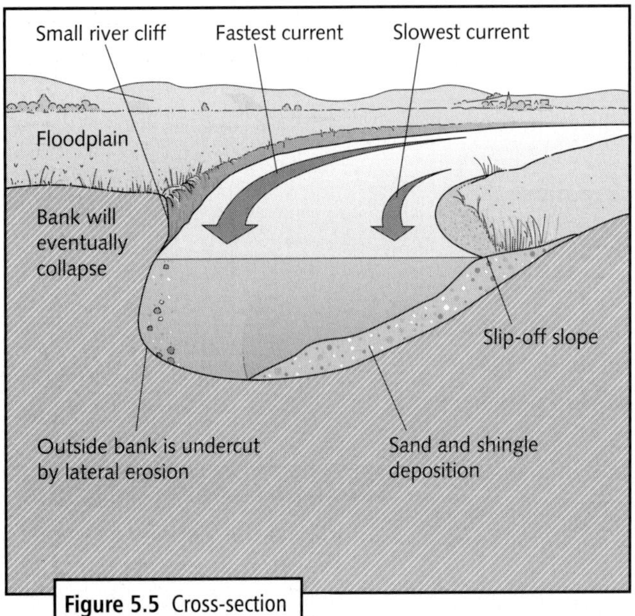

Back to …

The New Wider World
p284 Figure 17.16 for a photograph of a meandering river in East Sussex.

Small river cliff   Fastest current   Slowest current

Floodplain

Bank will eventually collapse

Slip-off slope

Outside bank is undercut by lateral erosion

Sand and shingle deposition

Figure 5.5 Cross-section of a meander

Floodplain and levées

The river widens its valley by lateral erosion. At times of high discharge, the river has considerable energy which it uses to transport large amounts of material in suspension. When the river overflows its banks it spreads out across any surrounding flat land causing flooding. The sudden increase in friction reduces the water's velocity and fine silt is deposited. Each time the river floods another layer of silt is added and a flat **floodplain** is formed (Figure 5.6). The coarsest material is dropped first and this can form a natural embankment, called a **levée**, next to the river. Sometimes levées are artificially strengthened to act as flood banks. If, during a later flood, the river breaks through its levées, then widespread flooding may occur.

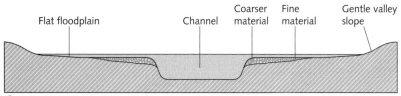

① **River in flood** – as the water flow slows, energy is lost. Coarser, heavier material is deposited on the bank and finer material further away.

② **River at low flow** – during a dry spell the river's velocity slows down and the volume falls. This causes material to be deposited on the bed.

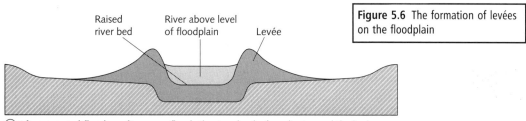

> **Figure 5.6** The formation of levées on the floodplain

③ **After repeated floods** – after many floods the river banks form levées and the bed may be raised so much that the river rises above the floodplain. This can lead to more flooding.

Deltas

As large rivers approach the sea, they have the energy to carry huge amounts of fine material in suspension. On reaching the sea, the river current may suddenly be reduced, allowing the material to be deposited. Sometimes deposition occurs in the main channel, and blocks it. The river has then to divide into a series of smaller channels, called distributaries, in order to reach the sea. Over a period of time the deposited material of sand and silt may build upwards and outwards to form a **delta**. Deltas are only likely to form where the amount of material brought down by a river is too great for sea currents to remove it (e.g. Mississippi and Ganges) or in seas that are virtually tideless (e.g. the Nile and Rhône in the Mediterranean). Deltas can also form when a river flows into the gentle waters of a lake.

Changes in the river channel

The river channel undergoes several distinct changes as it carries water from the source to the mouth of the river. These changes are summarised in Figure 5.7.

Figure 5.7 Changes in a river from source to mouth		Near source	Near mouth
RIVER CHANNEL	Width	Very narrow	Often very wide
	Depth	Shallow	Can be very deep
	Discharge	Small	Often very large
	Load	Small total	Large total

Back to ...

The New Wider World **p285** Figure 17.20 to look at the aerial photograph of the Mississippi delta.

Check this!...

1 Why does erosion occur on the outside of a meander?

2 Why do levées form directly beside the river?

3 Figure 5.1 on page 25 shows the rivers in Northern Ireland and the water areas into which they drain. Suggest why no deltas have formed at the mouth of these rivers.

4 Why do rivers increase in width between the source and the mouth?

3 Flood hazards can have physical and human causes

Causes of flooding

When the water within a river channel exceeds the capacity of the channel it will flood onto the surrounding land. It is important to understand that flooding is a normal occurrence in the lower course of a river and that is why the river creates its own floodplain. Floods become a hazard when the flow of water endangers people, property or natural environments.

Despite this danger, rivers throughout the world provide an attraction for human settlement and economic development. They provide:

- a water supply for domestic, industrial and agricultural use
- a source of power, food and recreation
- a means of transport.

However, under extreme climatic conditions, and increasingly due to human mismanagement, rivers can flood and cause death and widespread damage. Figure 5.8 lists some of the physical and human causes of flooding.

Back to ...

The New Wider World
pp286–289 for information on the causes and effects of the Lynmouth (England 1952) and Bangladesh (1998) floods.

Physical causes	Human causes
<ul><li>Long periods of continuous rainfall, e.g. Omagh flood (1987)</li><li>Intense rainfall caused by a thunderstorm: in summer the ground can be hard and dry, leading to increased surface runoff.</li><li>A sudden increase in temperature rapidly melts snow and ice in mountainous areas, e.g. the Himalayas or the Alps.</li><li>A monsoon climate – heavy rain occurs over a 4-month period.</li><li>Physical characteristics of the drainage basin, e.g. steep valley sides, will bring the water into the channel more quickly than gentle slopes.</li></ul>	<ul><li>Expansion of urban areas due to lack of planning controls. The impermeable coverings of tarmac and concrete and the drains associated with urban areas result in faster surface runoff, a shorter lag-time and a higher peak discharge.</li><li>The removal of trees (deforestation) reduces interception and increases surface runoff – this is a particular problem in LEDCs, e.g. Nepal where wood from trees represents the only source of energy.</li><li>Global warming is causing glaciers in the Himalayas to melt, which in turn increases surface runoff.</li><li>Rivers and streams can become blocked with waste and rubbish.</li><li>Disasters can occur when man-made features fail, e.g. a levée collapses or a dam bursts.</li></ul>

Figure 5.8 Physical and human causes of flooding

Impacts of flooding

When floods make the headlines in the media they are understandably portrayed in a negative light as the destructive forces of a river in flood can bring death, destruction and disruption to people's normal routines. However, as a geographer it is important that you consider all the possible impacts of flooding. The main impacts are summarised in Figure 5.9.

	Impact on people	Impact on the environment
POSITIVE	• Farming – deposition of silt acts as a natural fertiliser. • Rice growing is dependent on a certain amount of floodwater, e.g. Bangladesh. • Parasites that cause disease, e.g. Bilharziasis, can be flushed out of the river.	• Pollutants can be washed out of the river in a time of flood.
NEGATIVE	• Death • Injury • Loss of property (homes/businesses) • Cost of repairing damage and building/rebuilding defences • Inconvenience • Cost or availability of insurance • Disease, e.g. Hepatitis A, was a problem during the Mississippi floods of April 2001.	• Habitats on the river banks can be destroyed. • Stagnant water can be a breeding ground for mosquito larvae (dependent on climate) which carry diseases, e.g. malaria. **Figure 5.9** Impacts of flooding

Check this!...

1 Describe two physical and two human causes of flooding.

2 Using Figure 5.9, explain why flooding is referred to as a hazard.

4 Sustainable river management requires a co-ordinated approach

Key words to know

River management

River management is concerned with maximising the potential benefits of a river, e.g. transportation, power and recreation, whilst minimising the potential threat of flooding to human life and property.

Hard engineering measures

Traditionally, the flood hazard has been managed by hard engineering measures. This approach involves overcoming the natural processes in order to control the river and prevent the risk of flooding. Methods include:

- Building levées along the sides of the river or strengthening those that have formed naturally. These levées or embankments act to increase the capacity of the river channel and separate the river from its floodplain.
- Dredging the river bed in order to increase the capacity of the river channel. The deepening of the channel can also be achieved by building a groyne or wall across part of the channel. This increases the velocity of the water travelling through the remaining open section of the channel and this leads to erosion of the river bed.
- Straightening the course of the river. Water flows more quickly in a straight channel so the removal of meanders lessens the flood risk by allowing the water to leave that section of the river more quickly. However, this may simply move the flood risk to an area downstream. Continual maintenance is required to prevent the river from reverting to its natural course.

- Building a dam across the river can provide a means of controlling the discharge in the river. An additional economic benefit is that dams can also be used to generate hydro-electric power. However, the flooded area behind the dam may result in the displacement of large numbers of people, e.g. Three Gorges Dam on the Yangtze, or the destruction of sacred or historic sites, e.g. Aswan Dam on the Nile.

Soft engineering measures

Hard defences are not only very expensive to construct but they are also costly to maintain. For example, the maintenance work on the concrete levées of the Mississippi River (USA) costs $180 million every year. Towards the end of the twentieth century engineers began to question the use of hard engineering strategies as the sole method of managing the flood risk. A school of thought emerged which suggested that rather than tackling the problem of flooding, hard defences were contributing to it!

The soft engineering approach involves accommodation with the natural processes. Examples of these environmentally sensitive methods of flood control include:
- Building levées away from the channel to allow the river to flood onto at least part of the floodplain.
- Planting water-loving trees, e.g. willows, alongside the river. These plants will soak up water and reduce the amount of water in the soil.
- Afforestation – covering part of the drainage basin with trees which will intercept precipitation on their leaves and soak up water through their roots.
- Creating flood relief channels across the neck of meanders so that the river has the capacity to cope with an increased discharge when necessary.
- Establishing land use zones for the areas at risk. Those areas of the floodplain that are most at risk should only be used for non-essential activities, e.g. sports pitches.

The Rivers Agency is responsible for managing the drainage and flood defence aspects of Northern Ireland's network of watercourses. The Rivers Agency is part of the Department of Agriculture and Rural Development. Work is only carried out on approved or 'designated' watercourses, of which there are approximately 6800 km in Northern Ireland.

Part of the Agency's role is to implement flood alleviation schemes to protect urban areas where there is a threat to life or property. Two towns where such schemes have been put in place are Omagh and Castlederg. Due to historical development patterns on the floodplains in these towns, hard engineering measures such as concrete walls had to be put in place. Such walls have a detrimental effect on the environment by interfering with the natural processes of the river, so, in consultation with other relevant government departments and interest groups, the Rivers Agency seeks to limit environmental impact through a range of measures which include the planting of trees and improvement of fish habitats. This is an example of the co-ordinated approach that is necessary to ensure a sustainable future for the rivers in Northern Ireland.

Check this!...

1 Why do shipping companies favour the removal of meanders as a form of flood protection?

2 Describe an advantage of building levées away from the river channel.

River management on the Mississippi (USA)

Back to...

The New Wider World **p291** Figures 17.36 and 17.37 which present arguments for and against controlling rivers.

The Missouri River is the longest in the USA (3968 km) and a tributary of the Mississippi. The Mississippi–Missouri river system (Figure 5.10) is the fourth longest in the world (6019 km). In the summer of 1993 these rivers flooded causing the most devastating flood in US history. Approximately 3 billion cubic metres of water covered the floodplain north of St Louis and 44 000 km² of land were flooded in a region covering all or parts of nine states.

Figure 5.10 The area affected by the 1993 flood

Causes of the Mississippi–Missouri flood

The causes of the flooding are identified in Figure 5.11.

Impacts of the flood

- 28 lives lost
- 26 000 people evacuated
- 56 000 homes damaged
- Economic losses directly linked to the flood estimated at $10–12 billion
- 3 million hectares of farmland covered, destroying crops
- $500 million worth of damage to the road network

Management response to the flood

Following flood events in the 1930s the US Corps of Engineers worked to control flooding along the river by:

- building levées – to increase the capacity of the river
- straightening out meanders – to increase the velocity of water
- dredging the river – to increase the capacity of the river
- reinforcing the banks of the river with concrete (revetments) – to prevent erosion.

These measures were largely successful until 1993. Unfortunately, such measures cannot cope with the largest floods, which may only occur once in 100 years.

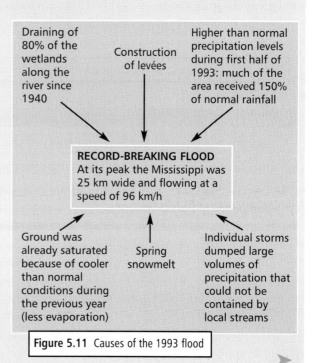

Figure 5.11 Causes of the 1993 flood

A co-ordinated approach for a sustainable future

The Mississippi–Missouri river system is an important resource for the United States but the devastation of the 1993 flood indicates that a more co-ordinated approach is required to ensure that future development of the river and its floodplain is sustainable. Co-ordination is more difficult where rivers cross interstate or international boundaries. Some of the demands that require management are shown in Figure 5.12.

There is some evidence that the first small step towards a more co-ordinated approach is taking place. The US Soil Conservation Service has spent $25 million on buying flood-prone farmlands for conversion to natural conditions, i.e. wetlands.

Rivers are dynamic systems which can never be fully controlled. It is only when we accept this and build this into the planning process that sustainable development will be assured.

Using your case study

Students need to be able to identify how the authorities have used hard and/or soft engineering measures to manage the river for human benefit. Students should also understand why a co-ordinated management approach is necessary for the sustainable development of the river and its floodplain.

Update

Go to *The NWW Coursemates* website for a link to the 'Rivernet' website which has information on management issues for the world's major rivers.

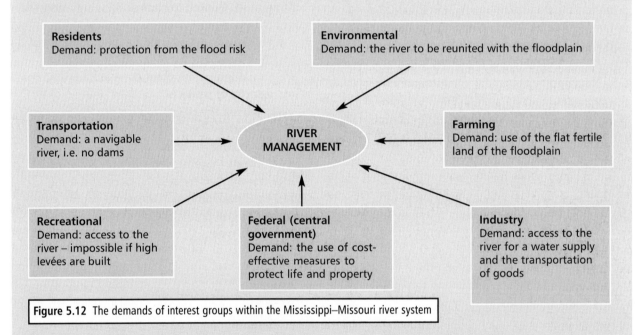

Figure 5.12 The demands of interest groups within the Mississippi–Missouri river system

---

Learn it!

1 Identify the physical and human causes of the 1993 Mississippi–Missouri flood.

2 Explain how the flood could result in economic losses of $10–12 billion.

3 Using Figure 5.12, explain why sustainable management of the river will require compromise by the various interest groups.

1 Using Figure 5.5, state one reason why deposition occurs on the inside of a meander. (3 marks)

2 Describe two hard engineering methods that could be used in the management of a river system. (4 marks)

3 For a named river management scheme you have studied, evaluate the success of the methods used to ensure sustainable development. (9 marks)

EXAM TIPS

The command word 'evaluate' in question 3 indicates that in order to gain maximum marks you need to consider any relevant strengths and weaknesses of the scheme in the context of sustainable development.

Back to ...

The NWW Coursemates website to check your answers to the exam practice question.

6
The management of limestone landscapes

KEY IDEAS

1 Rock structure and weathering combine to create a distinctive environment.

2 Limestone environments contain distinctive features.

3 Human pressures in limestone areas can lead to conflicts of interest.

Key words to know

Igneous rocks
Sedimentary rocks
Limestone
Metamorphic rocks

Back to ...

The New Wider World **p244**
Figures 15.1–15.4
which illustrate the rock types described above.

1 Rock structure and weathering combine to create a distinctive environment

Rock types and structures

The Earth's crust consists of many different types of rock. It is usual to group these rocks into three main types. This simple classification is based upon how each type of rock was formed.

- **Igneous rocks** result from volcanic activity. They consist of crystals which formed as the volcanic lava cooled down inside the volcano, e.g. granite (Mourne Mountains), or externally, e.g. basalt (North Antrim Hills).
- **Sedimentary rocks** have been laid down in layers and compressed by the weight of overlying sediment and water. They usually consist either of small particles that have been eroded and transported, e.g. sandstone and shale, or of the remains of plants and animals, e.g. **limestone** (Marble Arch, County Fermanagh), chalk (North Antrim coast) and coal.
- **Metamorphic rocks** are those that have been altered either by extremes of pressure, e.g. shale is compressed into slate, or by extremes of heat, e.g. limestone is changed into marble (white marble can be found on Rathlin Island).

Resistance

The structure of a rock can, among other things, affect its resistance to erosion and its permeability to water.

Rocks have different strengths and so produce different landforms. For example:

- The harder a rock is, the more resistant it is likely to be to the process of erosion. Harder rocks are therefore usually found as hills and mountains. The softer and less compact the rock, the more likely it is to be either broken up or worn away. Valleys are formed in softer rocks.
- In a drainage basin the more resistant the rock, the steeper the valley sides. Where resistant rock crosses a river's course, it is likely to create waterfalls and rapids.
- On coasts, resistant rocks form steep cliffs and stand out as headlands, whereas softer rocks form bays.

Permeability

An impermeable rock is one that does not let water pass through it, in contrast to a permeable rock which does allow water to pass through it. Permeable rocks may either:

- consist of tiny pores through which water can pass – such rocks, which include chalk, are said to be porous, or
- contain areas of weakness, such as bedding planes, along which water can flow.

Horizontal bedding planes, which separate individual layers of rock, can be seen in sandstone and Carboniferous limestone.

Rock structure, therefore, affects the landforms of an area and can produce distinctive types of scenery. This chapter focuses on the distinctive limestone scenery of the Marble Arch area of County Fermanagh.

Use of rocks

Many rocks have an important economic value. Such rocks are extracted, usually by mining or quarrying, for specific purposes, e.g. fireplaces and roofing slates.

Weathering

Rocks that are exposed on the Earth's surface become vulnerable to weathering. Weathering is the disintegration (breaking up) and decomposition (decay) of rocks *in situ* – that is, in their place of origin. Weathering, unlike erosion, need not involve the movement of material.

There are two main types of weathering:

- **Mechanical weathering** is the disintegration of rock into smaller pieces by physical processes without any change in the chemical composition of the rock. It is most likely to occur in areas of bare rock where there is no vegetation to protect the rock from extremes of weather. An example is **biological weathering** where tree roots penetrate and widen cracks in the rock until blocks become detached.
- **Chemical weathering** is the decomposition of rocks caused by a chemical change within the rock. It is more likely to occur in warm, moist climates, as these encourage chemical reactions to take place. An example of chemical weathering is limestone solution.

2 Limestone environments contain distinctive features

Limestone consists mainly of calcium carbonate. There are several types of limestone including Jurassic and Carboniferous limestone. Carboniferous limestone contains many fossils, including coral, indicating that it was formed on the bed of warm, clear seas.

Carboniferous limestone

Since its emergence from the sea, Carboniferous limestone has developed its own distinctive type of scenery, known as **karst**. Karst is the Slovenian word for dry, bare, shiny ground. The formation of karst landforms is dependent on the following factors.

Structure

Carboniferous limestone is a hard, grey sedimentary rock which was laid down in layers on the sea-bed. The horizontal junctions between the layers are called bedding planes. Joints are lines of weakness at right-angles to the bedding planes.

Permeability

Permeability is the rate at which water can either be stored in a rock or is able to pass through it. Chalk, which has many pore spaces, can store water and is an example of a porous rock. Carboniferous limestone, which lacks pore spaces, allows water to flow along the bedding planes and down the joints, and is an example of pervious rock.

Key words to know

Mechanical weathering
Biological weathering
Chemical weathering

Back to …

The New Wider World **p246** for further details on mechanical (physical) and chemical weathering.

Check this!.

1 Describe how sedimentary rocks form.

2 How can the resistance of rocks explain the formation of headlands and bays?

3 What is the difference between weathering and erosion?

4 Why are bare rocks most vulnerable to physical weathering?

Key words to know

Karst

Back to ...

Chapter 4 pages 19–21 for information on the moving continents.

Vulnerability to chemical weathering

Rainwater contains carbonic acid which is carbon dioxide in solution. Carbonic acid, although weak, reacts with calcium carbonate. The limestone is slowly dissolved by chemical weathering, and is then removed in solution by running water. Chemical weathering, therefore, widens weaknesses in the rock such as bedding planes and joints.

The limestone features of County Fermanagh

The limestone in this region was formed 354–290 million years ago when Ireland was submerged below a tropical sea, south of the Equator. It is possible to find fossils of animals that lived in this warm tropical sea.

Underground features

The most distinctive feature of limestone areas is the lack of surface drainage (Figures 6.1 and 6.2). The three rivers on the slopes of Cuilcagh Mountain (Owenbrean, Aghinrawn and the Sruh Croppa) flow over the surface until they reach an area of bare limestone. Various acids in the water, including carbonic acid derived from rainfall, have dissolved and widened surface joints to form **swallow holes**, or sinks. The rivers disappear down these swallow holes. Figure 6.2 shows two named swallow holes: Pollasumera and Pollreagh.

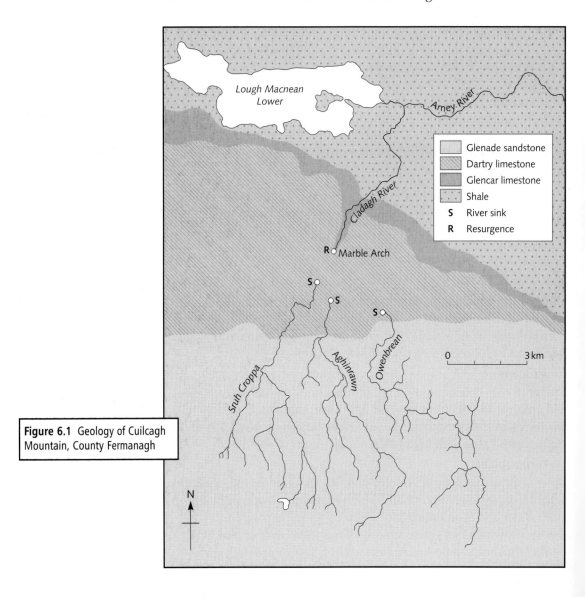

Figure 6.1 Geology of Cuilcagh Mountain, County Fermanagh

- Once underground, the rivers continue to widen joints and bedding planes through solution. This is how the passages in the Marble Arch Caves have formed over a period of time exceeding one million years. The rivers abandon these passages as they try to find a lower level. Within the **cave** system the three rivers join to form the Cladagh River.
- When the Cladagh River meets the underlying impermeable rock (Dartry limestone – an impure form of limestone), it flows over this rock until it reaches the surface as a spring, or resurgence. The water emerges at the top of the Cladagh Glen beside the arch after which the caves are named. Although the rock in the arch resembles marble because of its smooth, shiny appearance it is incorrectly named because it is made of limestone.

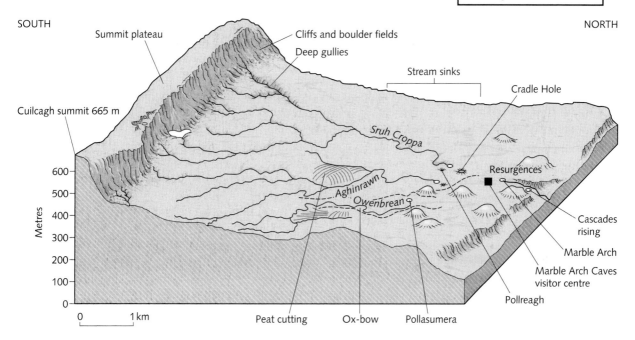

Figure 6.2 Limestone features of Cuilcagh Mountain

- Water, containing calcium carbonate in solution, continually drips from the ceilings of the underground caves or **caverns** (large caves) – Figure 6.3.
- Although it is cold in the caves, some evaporation does take place allowing the formation of icicle-shaped **stalactites** (Figure 6.3). A straw is a hollow type of stalactite. The largest stalactite in the caves is 2 metres long and is named after the French speleogist (speleology is the study of caves), Eduoard Martel, who was the first man to explore the caves in 1895. Curtains can form on the cave roof when calcite is deposited by water running down an inverted slope.
- As water drips onto the floor beneath the stalactite, further deposits of calcium carbonate produce the more rounded **stalagmites**. Pillars are the result of stalactites and stalagmites joining together. Other features on the cave floor include rimstone pools formed by the deposition of calcite on a rim by flowing water, and flowstones where calcite is deposited by water running over rocks.

Check this!...

1 What happens to a river when it reaches a swallow hole?

2 How do cave passages form?

Back to ...

The New Wider World **p249**
Figures 15.15–15.19 which
illustrate the surface
and underground features
described on pages 38–39.

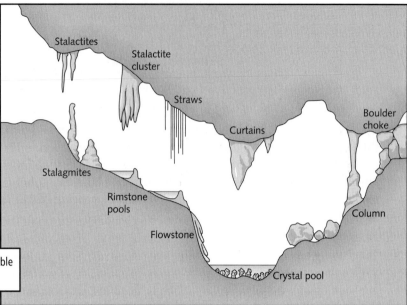

Figure 6.3 Limestone features of the Marble Arch Caves, County Fermanagh

Check this!...

1 Why do rivers not flow over exposed limestone rock?

2 With the aid of a simple diagram, explain the difference between a bedding plane and a joint.

3 Describe how a stalactite forms.

Surface features

- Limestone areas often have a flat, plateau-like appearance. The flatness is due to the underlying horizontal bedding planes. Where there is no soil, the top bedding plane is exposed as a **limestone pavement**. There are several good examples of limestone pavements within the Marlbank area.
- Many joints reach the surface along this pavement. They are widened and deepened by solution to form grooves known as **grykes**. The flat-topped blocks between grykes are called **clints**.

3 Human pressures in limestone areas can lead to conflicts of interest

Human activity can cause particular problems in limestone areas, which are scenically attractive.

Case Study Extra

Marble Arch Caves, County Fermanagh

Over the past 20 years human activity in this area of Northern Ireland has created pressures on the limestone environment in and around the Marble Arch Caves. These pressures and resulting impacts are listed in Figure 6.5.

Conflicts of interest

Given the wide range of demands placed upon this environment, it is perhaps not surprising that some of the activities are in conflict. Figure 6.6 shows some of the potential conflicts arising out of the various uses of this area.

Figure 6.4 The visitor centre at the Marble Arch Caves

Human pressures		Impacts
Tourists	In 1985 Fermanagh District Council (FDC) opened a part of the caves to the public as a tourist attraction at a cost of £1 million (Figure 6.4). Over 850 000 people have visited the caves since they opened.	• Economic benefits, e.g. jobs and tourist spending. • Increased traffic congestion on the narrow approach roads to the caves. • The improved level of access to the caves has also attracted unwanted visitors – in 1985 a group of vandals broke into the caves and threw stones at some of the features including the Martel stalactite which had to be repaired by renovation experts from the Ulster Museum.
Cavers	Before the show caves opened, an agreement was reached between the FDC and the Speleological Union of Ireland (SUI), which allowed sport cavers free access to the 42 km of caves.	• The increased numbers of novice cavers had become unsustainable by 1997. Large numbers of inexperienced cavers could inadvertently cause damage to the cave features.
Peat contractors	In the 1980s, 14 km of drains were dug to dry out parts of the blanket bog to allow extraction of the peat by mechanical peat cutters.	• Increased levels of surface runoff cause the caves to flood. • Reduced viability of the show caves as a tourist attraction under threat.
Farmers	Overgrazing of sheep on the slopes of Cuilcagh Mountain.	• Removal of the protective covering of vegetation on the peat bog, making it vulnerable to erosion.

Figure 6.5 Human pressures and impacts

Groups in conflict	Reasons
Visitors and landowners	• Visitors dropping litter. • Walking dogs in areas where sheep graze. • Visitors straying onto private land. • Traffic congestion (especially in July and August). • Moving animals could be a fraught operation with impatient tourists tooting horns and worrying sheep.
Farmers and FDC (the council that has operates the show) caves	• The land on the slopes of Cuilcagh Mountain limited uses; restricting sheep numbers could result in a fall of income for farmers. • For the caves to remain open, the vegetation on Cuilcagh requires protection.
Peat extractors and FDC	• Peat is a valuable resource in much demand by gardeners. However, extraction on this large scale and the subsequent flooding was threatening the future of the show caves.

Figure 6.6 Potential conflicts within the limestone environment of the Marble Arch Caves

Management response to the human pressures on the Marble Arch Caves

By the early 1990s it was clear that the pressures on the caves and on the surrounding area were not sustainable. Fermanagh District Council, in conjunction with a number of government departments, began to put in place a number of measures to protect this area for future generations (Figure 6.7).

In 2001 Marble Arch Caves and Cuilcagh Mountain Park were jointly awarded European Geo park status. Park manager, Richard Watson said, 'This new status is aimed at promoting an awareness of geology, sustainable tourism, good conservation and good education.'

A sustainable future?

In recent years weathered limestone has been removed from the Marlbank area for use by landscape gardeners. This area is unprotected and has yet to be designated an Area of Special Scientific Interest (ASSI). Therefore, although Fermanagh District Council has worked hard to balance its role as a tourism provider and a conservation manager, there is still work to be done in protecting this area, which is acknowledged as a national asset of international importance.

Using your case study

Use this case study to answer questions on the human pressures on a limestone environment

The Cuilcagh Mountain Park opened in 1999. The aims of this venture are to protect the intact areas of the bog, restore damaged areas and educate people on the value of the bog.

The bogland on Cuilcagh has been further protected through designation as an Area of Special Scientific Interest (ASSI) and an Environmentally Sensitive Area (ESA).

MANAGEMENT RESPONSE

Environmental protection staff from the DARD (Department of Agriculture and Rural Development) have been working with sheep farmers to encourage good conservation practices.

Potential conflicts between landowners and visitors have been largely alleviated by a road improvement scheme and by the opening of the mountain park which provides access for walkers.

Figure 6.7 Steps towards a sustainable future for the limestone environment of Cuilcagh and the Marble Arch Caves

within the British Isles. You will need to be able to identify the causes and impacts of the human pressure as well as the management response. Also use it for details of the conflicts of interest that can occur.

Case study links

The environmental problems associated with peat extraction are covered in more detail in Chapter 8 page 49.

Update

Go to *The NWW Coursemates* website for a link to the County Fermanagh web page. Click on the tourism link for more information on the Marble Arch Caves.

Learn it!

1 Explain why peat extraction threatened the future of the Marble Arch Caves.

2 Describe three impacts tourists could have on this environment.

3 With reference to Figure 6.7, identify the measure that you consider to be the most important in protecting this area for the future. Provide two reasons for your answer.

EXAM PRACTICE

1 Describe the processes that lead to the formation of a cave. (3 marks)

2 For a named area, explain fully two impacts of people on the limestone environment. (6 marks)

Back to ...

The NWW Coursemates website to check your answers to the exam practice question.

EXAM TIPS

To obtain the full 6 marks in question 2 it is essential that you make reference to the area you have studied and avoid making generalisations that may not be applicable to the area named.

Theme C: Ecosystems and Sustainability

The New Wider World, pp230–232

7 Local and global ecosystems

KEY IDEAS

1. Ecosystems are dependent on the interaction between climate, soil and vegetation.
2. Energy can be transferred within ecosystems through food webs.
3. Ecosystems operate at a range of scales.

Key words to know

Ecosystem
Flora
Fauna
Ecology
Soil

1 Ecosystems are dependent on the interaction between climate, soil and vegetation

An **ecosystem** is a natural system in which the life cycles of plants (**flora**) and animals (**fauna**) are closely linked to each other and to the non-living environment. Components of the living and non-living environment are shown in Figure 7.1. The study of the interrelationships found within an ecosystem is known as **ecology**.

Figure 7.1 Components of the living and non-living environments

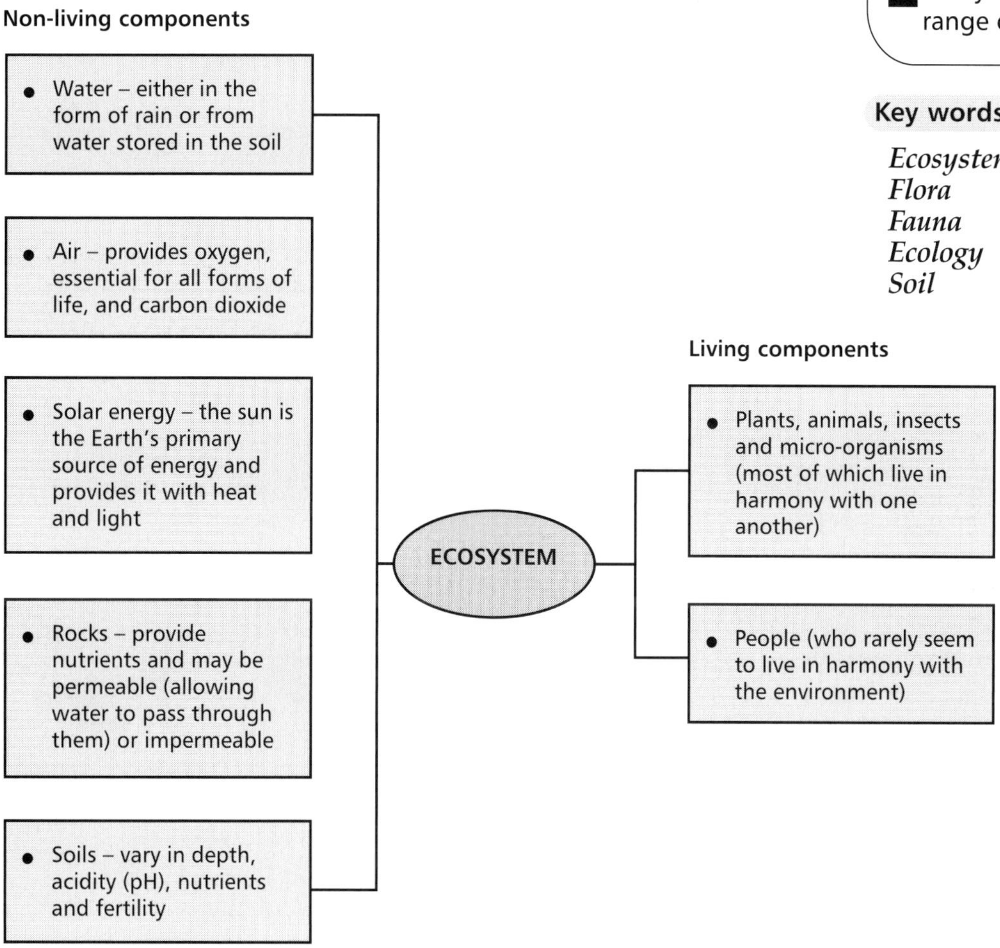
Non-living components
Water – either in the form of rain or from water stored in the soil
Air – provides oxygen, essential for all forms of life, and carbon dioxide
Solar energy – the sun is the Earth's primary source of energy and provides it with heat and light
Rocks – provide nutrients and may be permeable (allowing water to pass through them) or impermeable
Soils – vary in depth, acidity (pH), nutrients and fertility
ECOSYSTEM
Living components
Plants, animals, insects and micro-organisms (most of which live in harmony with one another)
People (who rarely seem to live in harmony with the environment)

The climate of any ecosystem will affect the formation of **soil**, the vegetation that will grow and the animal life it can support (Figure 7.2). Each component within the ecosystem depends upon, and influences, other components. For example, the climate affects the type of vegetation that will grow, while the vegetation may then begin to moderate the influence of climate on the ecosystem by providing shade or shelter.

Figure 7.2 The interrelated components within an ecosystem

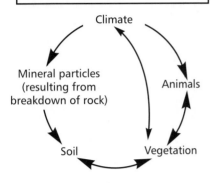

Climate

Mineral particles (resulting from breakdown of rock)

Animals

Soil

Vegetation

Key words to know

Producers
Consumers
Decomposers
Food web

2 Energy can be transferred within ecosystems through food webs

Any ecosystem depends upon two basic processes: the flow of energy and the recycling of nutrients.

- **Energy flows** Each ecosystem is sustained by the flow of energy through it. The main source of energy is sunlight which is absorbed by green plants and converted into food by the process of photosynthesis. Energy is then able to pass through the ecosystem in the food chain (Figure 7.3) in which plants are eaten by animals, and some animals consume each other. Food chains rarely contain more than six species because the amount of energy passed on diminishes at each stage.

- Even a small ecosystem, e.g. a pond, may contain many different species. Each species is usually involved in several different food chains. Therefore different food chains often interconnect to form a large network, called a **food web** (Figure 7.4).

Non-living environment →	Producers →	Consumers →	Consumers →	Decomposers →
– obtaining solar energy	– green plants which convert this energy by photosynthesis	– herbivores which eat green plants	– carnivores which consume herbivores	– e.g. bacteria which break down dead matter

Figure 7.3 Transfers of energy in an ecosystem

Figure 7.4 A food web for a tropical rainforest

Big cats ②   Eagles   Snakes

Pigs ②   Antelope   Monkeys   Birds   Frogs

Insects ②

Green plants ①

Snakes

Bacteria and fungi ③

Key
① Producers
② Consumers
③ Decomposers

Figure 7.5 The nutrient cycle

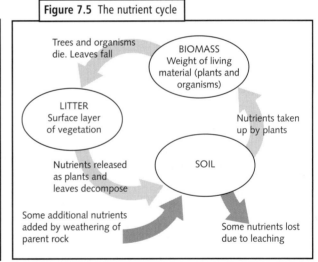

Trees and organisms die. Leaves fall

BIOMASS
Weight of living material (plants and organisms)

LITTER
Surface layer of vegetation

Nutrients taken up by plants

SOIL

Nutrients released as plants and leaves decompose

Some additional nutrients added by weathering of parent rock

Some nutrients lost due to leaching

Check this!...

1 What is an ecosystem?

2 Why is the number of species within a food chain limited?

3 Explain how nutrients can be retained within an ecosystem.

- **Recycling of nutrients** Certain nutrients are continually circulated within the ecosystem and so are part of a closed system. Each cycle involves plants taking up nutrients from the soil. The nutrients are then used by plants, or by animals which consume the plants. When the plants or animals die, they decompose and the nutrients are released and returned to the soil ready for future use (Figure 7.5).

Ecosystems can often be very fragile and some take hundreds of years to develop fully. They can, however, be irretrievably damaged in a short time by human activity, e.g. the tundra in Alaska, the Amazon rainforest and the peatlands of Europe.

44

3 Ecosystems operate at a range of scales

Ecosystems vary in size, from extensive areas of rainforest or grassland, to smaller areas of woodland and wetland, down to under a stone or within a droplet of water (Figure 7.6).

Level	Examples	
Micro	Water droplet	Under a leaf or stone
Meso (middle)	Freshwater pond	Woodland
	Sand-dunes	Hedgerows
	Salt marsh	Wetland
Macro (biome)	Tropical rainforest	Tropical grassland
	Coniferous forest	Tundra

Figure 7.6 Levels of ecosystems

Despite its relatively small geographical area, Northern Ireland contains a rich **biodiversity** (variety of living things) found in a number of ecosystems ranging from mountain bogs (e.g. Cuilcagh in County Fermanagh) to coastal sand-dunes (e.g. Magilligan, one of the largest dune systems in the British Isles).

At a global scale, a large ecosystem which contains the same type of vegetation, e.g. rainforest, is called a **biome**. Figure 7.7 shows the world biomes.

Figure 7.7 World biomes

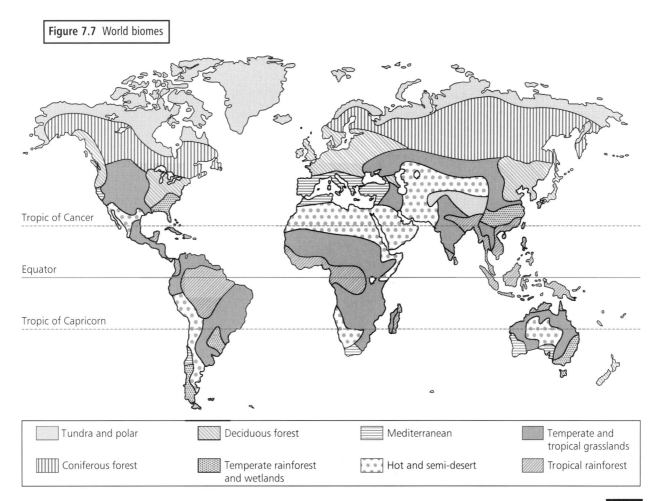

Tropic of Cancer

Equator

Tropic of Capricorn

- Tundra and polar
- Coniferous forest
- Deciduous forest
- Temperate rainforest and wetlands
- Mediterranean
- Hot and semi-desert
- Temperate and tropical grasslands
- Tropical rainforest

The bogs of Northern Ireland

Peat is found where slightly decomposed or entirely decomposed fibrous vegetable matter has formed a deep layer of soil under waterlogged conditions. A bog is a type of peatland that receives nutrients solely from precipitation rather than from rocks or groundwater. The locations of the main boglands are shown in Figure 7.8.

There are two types of bog:

- **Raised bogs** are typically found in the inland areas of Ireland where lake basins filled with partly rotted plants form fen peat, e.g. Ballynahone Bog, Country Londonderry. Bog moss then covers the fen as it is one of the few plants that can grow in the nutrient-deficient soil. Over thousands of years the peat slowly accumulates to rise above the surrounding land creating a raised bog. The sponge-like qualities of the mosses, e.g. Sphagnum, prevent water from draining away.

- **Blanket bogs** make up the largest percentage of peatlands in Northern Ireland e.g. Cuilcagh bog, County Fermanagh. Due to their extensive coverage, these bogs, which began to form over 5000 years ago, are known as 'blanket bogs'. They formed due to the leaching of iron down through the soil, which accumulated to form an impermeable layer called the iron pan. As precipitation could no longer drain away, the soil became saturated.

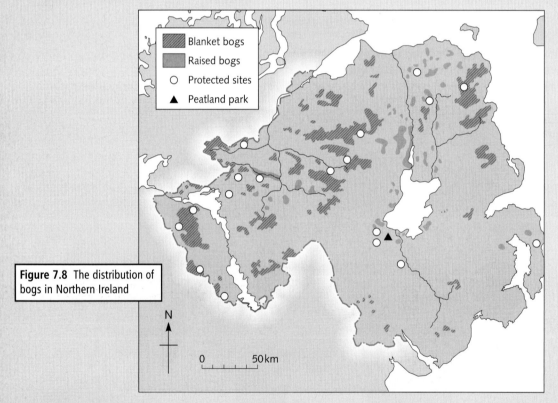

Figure 7.8 The distribution of bogs in Northern Ireland

Bogs are made up mostly of water (95–98 per cent), which contributes to that 'spongy' feeling experienced underfoot in these areas. The waterlogged conditions necessary for the formation of peat mean that decomposition takes places only very slowly (Figure 7.9).

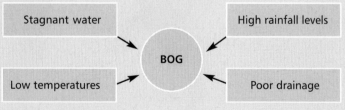

Figure 7.9 Necessary conditions for the creation of bogland

The lack of nutrients restricts the range of plant species found on the bogland. Spaghnum moss is one of the few plants that can grow in such harsh conditions because it requires few nutrients and can soak up water like a sponge. However, despite this lack of nutrients, bogs can still support complex food webs (Figure 7.10).

Some plants on the bog supplement their meagre supply of nutrients by eating insects! Butterwort is an example of a carnivorous plant – it has slippery leaves with edges that curve inwards: insects cannot crawl off, and become trapped to be slowly digested by glands on the leaf surface.

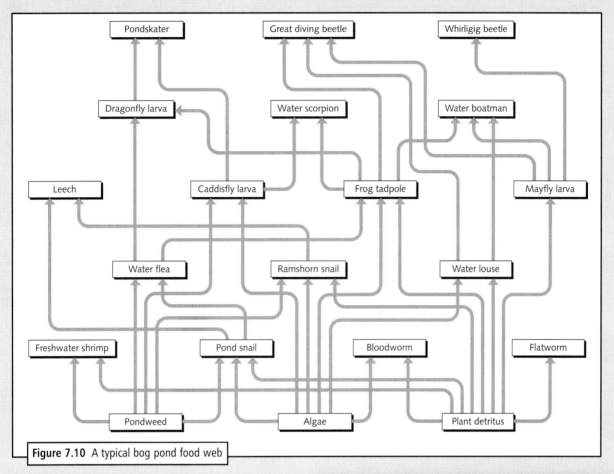

Figure 7.10 A typical bog pond food web

Using your case study
Use this case study as an example of a small-scale or local-scale ecosystem. You should understand:
- the distribution of bogs in Northern Ireland
- how this ecosystem has developed in response to the climatic and soil conditions.

Case study links
This case study links to the material in Chapter 8 pages 49 and 52 dealing with the human impacts on peatlands and conservation strategies.

Update
Go to *The NWW Coursemates* website for a link to the Irish Peatland Conservation Council website, which gives the latest news on peatland issues from around the world.

Learn it!

1 Name an area of blanket bog in Northern Ireland.

2 Describe how a blanket bog forms.

3 Use Figure 7.10 to identify two producers and two consumers found in a food web in a typical bog.

Case Study

The tropical rainforests

Back to...

The New Wider World **p232** for details on the structure of the tropical rainforest.

Using your case study

A tropical rainforest is an example of a global ecosystem. You should understand that these rainforests are found between the Tropics of Cancer (23½°N) and Capricorn (23½°S) – see Figure 7.7. They are located here because the hot (average temperature 27–30°C), moist (annual precipitation 2000–3000 mm) conditions give a year-round growing season resulting in prolific growth of vegetation. Examples include the Amazon (South America) and Congo (Africa) basins.

You should be aware that despite its lush appearance, the health of this biome is heavily dependent on the recycling of nutrients.

Although the forest topsoil is thin, the plants thrive because the nutrients from rotting leaves and vegetation are recycled so quickly.

Case study links

This case study links to the material in Chapter 8 pages 50, 53–54 dealing with the human impacts on tropical rainforests and conservation strategies.

Update

Go to *The NWW Coursemates* website for a link to 'Enchanted Learning', which gives details on the great diversity of plant and animal life found within this biome.

Learn it!

1 Describe the climate of the tropical rainforests.

2 List three ways in which the vegetation has adapted to the climate.

3 Explain why removal of the vegetation has a negative impact on the soil in this ecosystem.

EXAM PRACTICE

1 Study Figure 7.4 on page 44, which shows a food web for a tropical rainforest. State fully one effect on this ecosystem if the number of birds declined. (3 marks)

2 State the meaning of the term *biome*. (2 marks)

3 Using Figure 7.7 on page 45, identify the biome that dominates the British Isles. (1 mark)

4 The soils in the tropical rainforests contain few nutrients. Explain how the vegetation survives under these conditions. (5 marks)

Back to ...

The NWW Coursemates website to check your answers to the exam practice question.

EXAM TIPS

The Specification requires you to be able to locate and name world biomes. Therefore it is important that you are familiar with the biomes identified in Figure 7.7.

1 Human activities can have impacts on the soil, vegetation and animals within an ecosystem

Case Study Extra

Human activity on bogs in Northern Ireland

Bogland has been used as a resource for over 6000 years in Ireland but in recent decades human activity has had a detrimental impact on the sensitive balance of this ecosystem.

- **Drainage** Large areas of blanket bog were drained in the 1950s and 1960s to create new areas of pasture for livestock. Large areas have also been drained to dry out the bog in preparation for peat extraction. This can lead to:
  – a reduction in biodiversity
  – a loss of habitats
  – greater surface run off increasing the risk of flooding.

- **Peat extraction** Peat has been used as a source of fuel in Ireland since the 1600s, and in Northern Ireland 77.5 per cent of raised bogs have been cut for fuel. The horticultural industry and amateur gardeners have created a new and lucrative market for peat. Combined with the introduction of mechanical peat cutters, this has resulted in the rapid removal of large areas of peatland – a process known as peat milling (Figure 8.1). This severe human impact removes the soil and vegetation resulting in a loss of animal habitats.

Figure 8.1 Peat milling

- **Grazing** When the UK joined the EU in 1973, farmers in Northern Ireland became eligible for a range of financial incentives which boosted the number of cattle and sheep. This had the effect of increasing the use of blanket bog for rough grazing and resulted in:

KEY IDEAS

1 Human activities can have impacts on the soil, vegetation and animals within an ecosystem.

2 Conservation of ecosystems can bring many benefits.

Key words to know

Afforestation

– a reduction in surface vegetation, e.g. heather
– exposure of the peat soil leaving it vulnerable to erosion.

- **Afforestation** Up until the 1980s the Forestry Service viewed blanket bogs as being suitable for tree planting because the land had a low commercial value and there was plenty of it. This resulted in approximately 20 per cent of Northern Ireland's blanket bogs being lost to afforestation. This can affect the ecosystem by:
  – increasing surface run-off through drainage
  – covering over feeding and nesting grounds of birds, e.g. red grouse.

Using your case study

Use this case study to answer questions on the impact of human activities on a peatland ecosystem in Northern Ireland.

Case study links

Refer to Chapter 6 pages 40–42 for details on the extraction of peat from Cuilcagh Mountain. This case study also links to the case study on pages 52–53.

Learn it!

1 Describe the impact of grazing on peatland soil.

2 Explain why the removal of peat may have an impact outside the area of extraction.

Deforestation in the Amazon basin

Deforestation

Although one-third of the world's trees still grow in the Brazilian rainforest, their numbers are being rapidly reduced through the deliberate clearing of large areas by cutting or burning. This process is called **deforestation**. According to the WWF (World Wide Fund for Nature), 22 hectares of rainforest are lost *every minute* to deforestation. That's the equivalent of one football field every two seconds!

Year	Population
1900	17.4 million
1950	51.9 million
1970	93.1 million
2000	169.0 million

Figure 8.2 Brazil's population growth

Causes of deforestation

Brazil's rapid population growth since the 1960s (Figure 8.2) has necessitated the following:

- more land for people to live on
- more farmland to produce food for the extra numbers
- more jobs for people to earn a living
- more resources, if people's standard of living was to improve.

The exploitation of the Brazilian rainforest, at that time largely undeveloped, offered a ready-made solution to these problems, as well as an opportunity to reduce the country's huge national debt.

The destruction of the tropical rainforests in the Amazon basin has centred on four activities (Figure 8.3).

Figure 8.3 Causes of deforestation

Population growth

↓

Resource shortage

↓

Exploitation of rainforest (deforestation)

Communications
- 12 000 km of new roads
- Railways (Carajas–São Luis)
- Airstrips

Settlement
- Towns and cities have been built to house the expanding population, e.g. Maraba (150 000)

Timber/mineral/water resources
- Hardwoods and minerals, e.g. bauxite and iron are valuable exports
- Hydro-electric power offers a cheap source of electricity

Farming
- 'Slash and burn' (see text)
- Subsistence farming has supported many of the new arrivals
- Cattle ranches operate to serve overseas markets

Back to...

The New Wider World p237 Figure 14.24 which illustrates the location of some of the human activities in the rainforest.

Impacts of deforestation

Leaching
Erosion

The destructive impact of human activity on the soil, vegetation and animals can be seen clearly by examining the practices involved in 'slash and burn' agriculture and timber logging.

- 'Slash and burn' agriculture was originally used by native Indians to grow crops like manioc (tapioca). The area cleared was small and it was only cultivated for two or three years before the tribe moved on, allowing the rainforest to recolonise the area. Since the 1960s vast areas have been cleared by the use of firebombs dropped from the air, and defoliants – chemicals that strip the trees bare. The trees dry out in the sun and can quickly burn into a firestorm consuming all the remaining creatures. It is estimated that 137 plant, animal and insect species are lost every single day due to deforestation.

The areas cleared are too large for the forest to recover. Heavy rains wash the nutrients out of the soil, a process known as **leaching**. The soil quickly loses its fertility and therefore any agricultural value.

- Logging companies are only interested in certain species of tree to meet the overseas demand for hardwoods, e.g. teak and mahogany. Forestry products generate US$20 billion annually. In order to reach these trees all the others have to be felled and cleared. This breaks the nutrient cycle (Figure 7.5, page 44) leaving the soil vulnerable to **erosion** from the heavy tropical downpours.

Using your case study

Use this case study to answer questions on the impact of human activities on an area of tropical rainforest at the regional (Amazon basin) or national (Brazil) scale.

Case study links

This case study links with the case study on the conservation of tropical rainforests on pages 53–54.

Update

Go to *The NWW Coursemates* website for a link to the Brazil web page and follow the link 'Brazil in the schools' (secondary).

Learn it!

1 Give two reasons why deforestation has occurred in the Amazon basin.

2 Explain how farming has contributed to deforestation.

3 Why does deforestation lead to a decline in soil fertility?

---

2 Conservation of ecosystems can bring many benefits

Key words to know

Conservation

Environmental protection groups including Friends of the Earth, WWF and Greenpeace are involved in publicising the many benefits of conserving fragile environments and protesting against their destruction (Figure 8.4). **Conservation** involves protecting areas under threat and identifying ways in which sustainable development can be achieved.

Figure 8.4 Action outside a furniture shop in London in protest against the illegal import of timber from the Indonesian rainforests (January 1999)

Protecting the peatlands of Northern Ireland

By 2003, thirteen areas of bog were designated as Special Areas of Conservation (SAC) but as recently as the 1980s the protection of bogland was not regarded as a priority by government agencies. The case of Ballynahone Bog demonstrates how attitudes towards bogland conservation have changed in recent decades.

Ballynahone Bog

Ballynahone Bog is a raised bog situated near Maghera in County Londonderry. Formed in the valley of the Moyola River which flows into Lough Neagh, it is one of the two largest intact active bogs in Northern Ireland and its layers contain evidence of changes in the local vegetation and climate.

The bog provides an important habitat for breeding birds, e.g. the curlew, and for wintering species such as the merlin and various ducks. The peatland flora includes a number of rare species, including bog-rosemary – Ballynahone Bog is one of only four known sites in Northern Ireland where this grows.

- **Exploitation of the bog** The Bulrush Peat Company purchased the bog in 1980 for development as a source of horticultural peat. In 1987 the company made a planning application to install drains in the bog the following year. This would allow the bog to dry out before the extraction of peat would begin in 1994. Despite many objections from naturalists, local people and the Department of the Environment Countryside and Wildlife Branch, planning permission was granted in August 1988 as the planning commissioner was aware that the surface of the bog was already drying out as a result of previous peat extraction and he did not believe that this process could be halted and reversed. By 1990 21 km of drains had been excavated in preparation for peat excavation.
- **Bringing the bog back to life** Dismayed by the destruction of the bog, a local pressure group, Friends of Ballynahone Bog (FBB),

was formed to try and reverse the planning decision. The group enlisted the help of the television presenter Professor David Bellamy and Friends of the Earth to publicise their cause.

Figure 8.5 FBB campaign poster

With the environmental lobby gaining strength, the planning permission was revoked and the first step in reversing the damage caused by the drains could proceed. Dams were placed across the drains to allow the bog to recharge with water and return it to life.

The value of the bog has been recognised in the following designations:
- 1995: Area of Special Scientific Interest
- 1998: RAMSAR site – recognising the area as a wetland of international importance
- 2000: Special Area of Conservation – designed to protect the most threatened habitats in Europe.

The future for the bog....

The long-term future of the bog was made secure in 1997 when the Environment and Heritage Service (EHS) agreed to purchase the bog from the Bulrush Company for £2 million.

The management of the bog is now carried out by a committee made up of representatives from the Ulster Wildlife Trust, Environment and Heritage Service and the Friends of Ballynahone Bog.

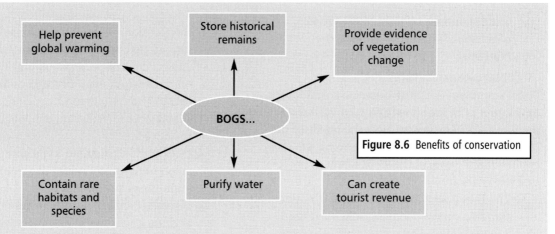

Figure 8.6 Benefits of conservation

BOGS...

- Help prevent global warming
- Store historical remains
- Provide evidence of vegetation change
- Contain rare habitats and species
- Purify water
- Can create tourist revenue

The benefits of conservation

The remaining boglands of north-west Europe have been compared with the tropical rainforest in terms of their global importance. Conservation ensures that the ecosystem can continue to function while bringing a range of benefits (Figure 8.6).

Using your case study

Use this case study to answer questions on the benefits of conservation to the soil, the vegetation, the animals and the local communities.

Case study links

This case study links to the case study on the impact of human activities on a peatland ecosystem in Northern Ireland on page 49.

Update

Go to *The NWW Coursemates* website for a link to Geography in Action which provides more details on Ballynahone Bog.

Learn it!

1 Why was Ballynahone Bog under threat in the 1980s?

2 State fully three reasons why people campaigned to protect the bog.

Protecting the rainforests in the Amazon basin

The benefits of conservation

The benefits of conserving the rainforests are not limited to the population of the area. The global population can benefit as the trees absorb carbon dioxide, thereby slowing down the process of global warming. The dense vegetation contains many benefits for humans. For example:

- Only 7 per cent of all the plants have been tested for potential human uses; 650 species of plant with pharmaceutical and economic value have been assessed. One medicine already in use is hydrocortisone which is used to treat inflammation and arthritis.
- 48 native fruits of the Amazon have been identified as having potential for sale on the international market, including fruit juice from the Acai palm tree.
- New foods are also discovered every day, like the naranjilla which looks like a fuzzy tomato but tastes like a strawberry/ pineapple.
- Products from the rainforests provide 80 per cent of the world's dietary range, from nuts to citrus fruits.
- The biodiversity is of great interest to scientists. It is estimated that 10–15 per cent of all living species live here. A single pond in the rainforest can sustain a greater variety of fish than are found in all of Europe's rivers.
- There is much potential for the growth of ecotourism in this region, which could

➤ bring economic benefits to the local population without destroying the rainforest.

Conservation measures

Brazil's problem is how to organise sustainable development in such a way that the resources of the forest are exploited to meet the needs of the 20 million inhabitants without harming the environment. Some of the steps taken over the past ten years are listed below:

- The Forest Stewardship Council (FSC) has started a certified logging scheme (Figure 8.7) to promote the sustainable use of the forest.
- The inclusion of mahogany in the Convention on the International Trade of Threatened Species (CITES) in 2003 means stricter control over the export of Brazilian mahogany. All export countries must demonstrate that wood has come from sustainable forests and been legally produced.
- In 1997 Brazil pledged to protect at least 10 per cent of forests under the 'Forests for Life' initiative of WWF.
- Forest fires are now monitored by satellite and the government has implemented programmes in the areas of prevention, control, combat and training.

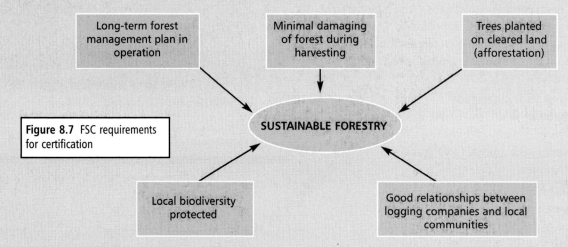

Figure 8.7 FSC requirements for certification

A sustainable future?

Despite the measures described above, figures published in June 2003 by the National Space Research Institute of Brazil (INPE), estimate that 25 476 km^2 were deforested between August 2001 and August 2002 – an increase of 40 per cent on the previous period, when the area deforested was estimated at 18 166 km^2. It is clear that much still has to be done to protect this valuable biome.

Using your case study

Use this case study to answer questions on the benefits of conservation to the soil, the vegetation, the animals and the local communities.

Case study links

This case study links to the case study on the impact of human activities in the rainforests on pages 50–51.

Update

Go to *The NWW Coursemates* website for a link to the Brazil web page. Click on 'environment' and then on 'Amazonia' or 'Forests and Forestry'.

Learn it!

1 Identify two benefits of conserving the rainforest.

2 Describe three measures used to protect the tropical rainforests.

1 a Name a peatland ecosystem within Northern Ireland that you have studied. (1 mark)

  b For the ecosystem named in (a), describe one impact of human activity on the ecosystem. (2 marks)

2 Define the term *deforestation*. (2 marks)

3 Explain fully two reasons why deforestation is occurring in the tropical rainforests. (6 marks)

4 Describe three benefits of conserving the tropical rainforests. (6 marks)

EXAM TIPS

To gain maximum marks for question 3, ensure that you include a named example of a tropical rainforest that you have studied.

Back to ...

The NWW Coursemates website to check your answers to the exam practice question.

9 Sustainable management of ecosystems

KEY IDEAS

1 The tropical grasslands show the effect of climate on vegetation.

2 Ecotourism can contribute to sustainable development.

Key word to know

Savanna

◄ **Back to ...**

Chapter 7, page 45, Figure 7.7 for the location of the savanna grasslands.

1 The tropical grasslands show the effect of climate on vegetation

Savannas, or tropical grasslands, are one of the world's major ecosystems or biomes covering large areas of sub-Saharan Africa, South America and northern Australia. The vegetation in this biome is made up of tall grasses, scattered trees and bushes.

Climate

The climate data in Figure 9.1 provides evidence of the two distinct seasons that influence this biome – the wet and the dry seasons.

Vegetation

Where the savanna merges with the tropical rainforest, the vegetation is dense woodland with patches of tall grass. Moving away from these margins, the vegetation slowly changes to typical savanna grasslands with scattered trees (rain for half the year), and eventually to the drought-resistant bushes and odd clumps of grass on the desert margins (hardly any rain).

During the dry season the landscape turns brown in the heat, and fire can spread easily, but in the wet season the vegetation comes back to life. The vegetation responds to these distinct seasons, as shown in Figure 9.2.

Figure 9.1 Climate figures for Niamey (Niger, Africa), latitude 13°N, longitude 2°E												
Month	Jan	Feb	Mar	Apr	May	Jun	Jul	Aug	Sep	Oct	Nov	Dec
Precipitation (mm)	0.2	0.0	3.2	6.0	34.6	74.6	143.4	187.3	90.3	15.7	0.5	0.0
Av. temperature (°C)	24.2	27.1	30.8	33.7	33.9	31.3	28.8	27.5	28.5	30.5	27.9	24.8

◄ **Back to ...**

The New Wider World **p233** Figure 14.13 for a picture of the savanna vegetation.

Figure 9.2 The response of vegetation to the savanna climate

Dry season
- Deciduous trees turn yellow
- Grasses turn yellow and dry up
- Some trees shed their leaves while others produce thorn-like leaves to reduce transpiration
- Most plants are drought-resistant with long roots to reach underground water supplies
- The baobab tree has a thick bark and stores water in its trunk
- Trees like the acacia are fire-resistant

Wet season
- Grasses grow quickly in the hot, wet conditions
- The grasses flower and produce new seeds
- Trees produce new leaves

Animals also adapt to the contrasting seasons. Many migrate during the dry season to find food and return again when the rains come.

The savanna ecosystem under threat

The relationships between the savanna climate, vegetation and animal life are shown in Figure 9.3.

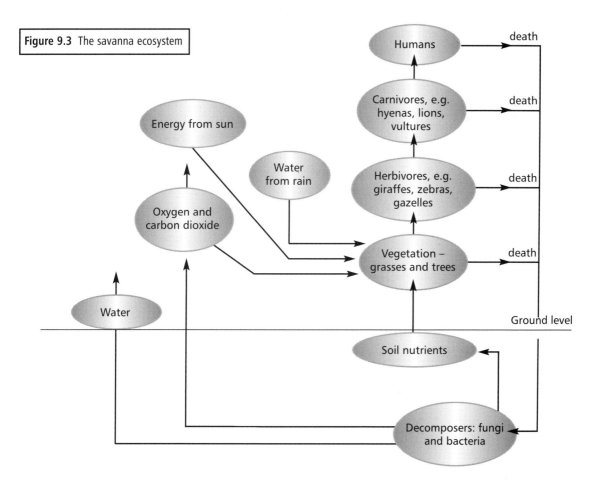

Figure 9.3 The savanna ecosystem

This large-scale ecosystem or biome is under threat in many parts of the world due to population pressure. Population pressure leads to more farming on the savanna which has negative impacts on the soil, vegetation and animal life:

- wells are drilled allowing more animals to be kept but this can lead to overgrazing
- overgrazing leaves the soil exposed and vulnerable to erosion by wind and rain
- wild animals are pushed into smaller areas which in turn puts more pressure on the vegetation.

2 Ecotourism can contribute to sustainable development

The conservation of the savanna grasslands has proved difficult due to the population pressures that exist in many of the countries in which they are found. The majority of these countries are LEDCs and therefore economic development and meeting the basic needs of the population are considered of greater importance than conservation. The attraction of earning money from tourism is considerable to less

Check this!...

1 Use Figure 9.1 to identify which months make up the dry and wet seasons.

2 Describe two ways in which trees within this ecosystem adapt to the climate.

3 Explain how human activity is threatening to turn large parts of the savanna into desert.

Key word to know

Ecotourism

Back to ...

The New Wider World **p168** Figure 10.23 for examples of tourism in LEDCs.

Check this!...

1 Identify three benefits of ecotourism for the environment.

2 Why can eotourism create probems for the Maasai people?

economically developed countries, many of which see it as the only possible way to raise their standard of living. However, the tourist industry can have negative impacts on the local culture and the environment.

One way of resolving this conflict between conservation and development could be the promotion of **ecotourism**, which includes:

- visiting places in order to appreciate their scenery and wildlife and to understand their culture
- creating economic opportunities (jobs) in an area while at the same time protecting natural resources (scenery and wildlife) and the local way of life (culture).

Kenya is a good example of an LEDC that has embraced the concept of ecotourism. The Kenyan authorities have set up over 50 National Parks and game reserves to protect and manage its environment, hoping to gain economic benefits that come from tourists wishing to visit these areas. Tourism has become Kenya's major source of overseas income, with over one million tourists a year. The opportunity of observing 'the big five' (i.e. lions, leopards, buffalo, elephants and rhino) in close proximity is a major attraction for tourists but the impact of their visit on the local population and the ecosystem is not always positive (Figure 9.4).

	Advantages	Disadvantages
Local communities	• Maasai and their settlements used as tourist attractions – income helps to improve their living standards. • Traditional culture and skills are retained – for the tourists and future generations of Maasai.	• Nomadic communities displaced when reserves set up – loss of dignity and traditional ways. • Alcohol and exposure of the body offend Muslim communities. • Loss of large chunks of grazing land. • Financial dependency on foreign tourists.
Vegetation	• Profits from ecotourism can be invested in protecting the vegetation – replanting of acacia trees. • Reserves allow endangered species to thrive.	• Too many tourist minibuses destroy grasses when they drive off-road to get close to game. • Upset camping stoves cause many bush fires.
Animals	• Animals can live and breed in protected areas. • Poaching of wild animals is reduced as numbers of tourists increase in the park.	• Hot air balloons for tourist trips frighten animals. • Too many tourists interrupt the breeding cycles of rare animals.
Soil	• Profit from tourism can encourage better farming practices in the nearby highland arable areas. • Protected areas allow soils to develop naturally.	• Tourist minibuses compact the soil and prevent drainage, resulting in soil erosion in the wet season. • Less mobility by the Maasai herds leads to overgrazing and desertification.

Figure 9.4 The advantages and disadvantages of ecotourism

Ecotourism in Kenya

Back to...

The New Wider World **pp170–171** for details of tourism in Kenya.

Key word to know

Sustainable

The Amboseli National Park opened in 1974. It is situated in the foothills of Mount Kilimanjaro, 135 km from the capital Nairobi, and covers 392 km². It is one of over 50 parks and game reserves that have been established to protect the environment and generate tourist revenue. Unfortunately the Maasai herders (Figure 9.5) who had lived in harmony with nature for over 400 years were forced off the land, creating much resentment.

Figure 9.5
A Maasai herder

As tourist numbers grew to over 150 000 per year during the 1990s, the environment began to suffer. Vehicles left the tracks to get close to the animals, disturbing them and damaging the vegetation.

Kimana Wildlife Sanctuary

In response to the problems occurring in Amboseli, Kimana Sanctuary was established in 1992 with funding from the USAID Conservation of Bio-diverse Areas project and the Kenyan Government. Officially opened in 1996, the sanctuary gained international recognition for being the first-ever community wildlife sanctuary in Africa. The benefits to the local community and the environment were clear:

- Money from gate collections was allocated to community, educational and health projects.
- Kimana has its own warden, local scouts, and workers – providing much needed employment for the community.
- As the local people now depend on the wildlife for income from tourism, they have a greater interest in conserving the environment.

The Kenyan experience proves that tourism occurring in the natural environment does not always equate with environmentally friendly tourism, or ecotourism. There is a general reluctance to limit the growth of tourism in Kenya because it is so important to the economy (138 000 jobs and 360 000 people in indirect employment) but this attitude could ultimately destroy the ecosystem on which the tourist industry depends. The Kimana Wildlife Sanctuary demonstrates that ecotourism can be a **sustainable** form of development for LEDCs.

Using your case study

Use this case study as an example of ecotourism. You should understand that although ecotourism can bring many benefits this is not always the case in reality. Make sure you can explain how in this case ecotourism can be a sustainable form of development for LEDCs.

Update

Go to *The NWW Coursemates* website for a link to the United Nations' guidelines on ecotourism. See also other links to The International Ecotourism Society and Ecobrazil.

Learn it!

1 Why is the savanna ecosystem in Amboseli under threat?

2 Identify two ways in which Kimana Wildlife Sanctuary represents a sustainable form of ecotourism.

1   Study Figure 9.3 on page 57. Describe
    two possible impacts on this ecosystem
    if the vegetation were removed
    through overgrazing.   (4 marks)

2   Define the term *ecotourism*.   (2 marks)

3   'Ecotourism cannot meet the needs of
    tourists in a way that is friendly to the
    environment and the local culture.'
    Discuss this statement with reference
    to a named case study.   (6 marks)

Back to ...

The NWW Coursemates
website to check your
answers to the exam
practice question.

EXAM TIPS

In order to gain maximum marks in question 3, remember to
show the examiner that you are aware that there is more than
one side to the issue.

⇨ *The New Wider World*, pp4–5

10 Population distribution and density

1 Population distribution and density tend to be uneven

Distribution describes the way in which people are spread out across the Earth's surface. This distribution is uneven and changes over periods of time. It is usual to show population distribution by means of a dot map (Figure 10.1). The dot map shows the population spread across the world but settlements with fewer than 100 000 people are not shown. Notice how people are concentrated into certain parts of the world, making those places very crowded. These areas include **million cities** – cities with a population of one million people or more. Some of these cities are marked on Figure 10.1 At the same time, other areas have relatively few people living there. These are said to be sparsely populated.

KEY IDEAS

1 Population distribution and density tend to be uneven.

2 Physical and human factors can affect population distribution and density.

Key words to know

Distribution
Million cities
Density
High population density
Low population density

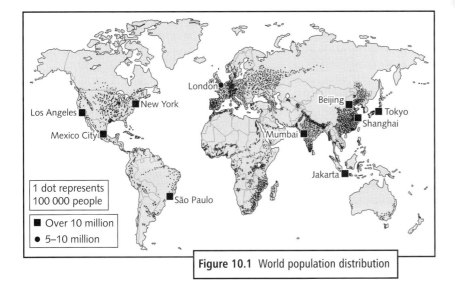

1 dot represents 100 000 people

■ Over 10 million
● 5–10 million

Figure 10.1 World population distribution

Density describes the number of people living in a given area, usually a square kilometre (km²). Density is found by dividing the total population of a place by its area. Population density is usually shown by a choropleth map (Figure 10.2). A choropleth map is easy to read as it shows generalisations, but it does tend to hide concentrations. For example:

- The UK appears to have a **high population density** but in reality some parts are more crowded than others (Figure 10.3).
- Brazil appears on the world map in Figure 10.2 to have a **low population density**. However, in reality several parts of the country have very high densities, e.g. Rio de Janeiro and São Paulo.
- Figure 10.2 suggests that the population of Egypt is evenly spread whereas in reality it is concentrated along the Nile Valley (Figure 10.1).

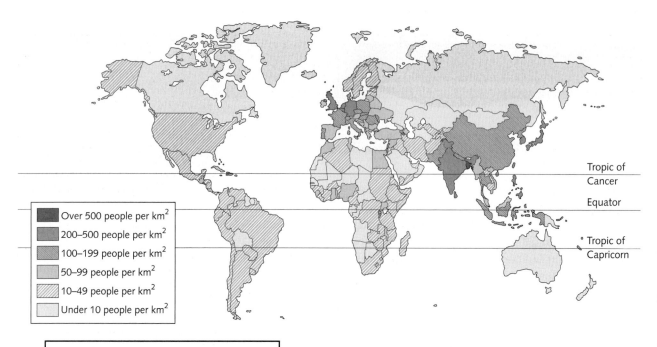

| Over 500 people per km^2 |
| 200–500 people per km^2 |
| 100–199 people per km^2 |
| 50–99 people per km^2 |
| 10–49 people per km^2 |
| Under 10 people per km^2 |

Tropic of Cancer

Equator

Tropic of Capricorn

Figure 10.2 World population density by country

Figure 10.3 Variations in population density within the UK

Country	Population density
Scotland	64 people per km^2
Northern Ireland	119 people per km^2
Wales	139 people per km^2
England	376 people per km^2

Check this!...

1 What is the difference between population distribution and density?

2 Why is a choropleth map unsuitable for displaying population distribution?

2 Physical and human factors can affect population distribution and density

Key word to know

Relief

On global and continental scales, patterns of distribution and density are mainly affected by physical factors such as **relief** (the height and shape of the land), climate, vegetation, soils, natural resources and water supply. At regional and more local scales, patterns are more likely to be influenced by human factors which may be economic, political or social. Figure 10.4 gives reasons, with specific examples, why some parts of the world are densely populated while others are sparsely populated.

PHYSICAL				
	Densely populated	**Examples**	**Sparsely populated**	**Examples**
Relief	Flat plains and low-lying undulating areas	Bangladesh	High, rugged mountains	Andes
Climate	Evenly distributed rainfall with no temperature extremes	North-west Europe	Limited annual rainfall	Sahara Desert
	Areas with (i) high sunshine totals (ii) heavy snowfall for tourism	(i) Spanish costas (ii) Swiss Alpine valleys	Low annual temperatures High annual humidity	Greenland Amazon rainforest
Vegetation	Grasslands – easy to clear/farm	Paris basin	Forest	Amazonia, Canadian Shield
Soil	Deep fertile silt left by rivers	Nile valley and delta	Thin soils in mountainous or glaciated areas	Northern Scandinavia
Natural resources	Minerals, e.g. coal, iron ore	Pennsylvania, Johannesburg	Lacking minerals	Ethiopia
Water supply	Reliable supplies	North-west Europe	Unreliable supplies	Afghanistan
HUMAN				
	Densely populated	**Examples**	**Sparsely populated**	**Examples**
Economic	Ports	New York, Sydney	Limited facilities for ports	Bangladesh
	Good roads, railways, airports	Germany, California	Poor transport links	Himalayas
	Money available for new high-tech industries	California, south of France	Lack of money for new investments	Nepal, Gaza
Political	Government investment	Tokyo region, north Italy	Lack of government investment	Dem. Rep. of the Congo
Social	Better housing opportunities	Arizona	Poor housing opportunities	Afghanistan, Soweto

Figure 10.4 Factors affecting distribution and density of population

Case Study Extra

Population density in Sweden

Sweden is an EU member state located in northern Europe on the Scandinavian peninsula. Its population characteristics are compared with those of Northern Ireland in Figure 10.5.

Figure 10.5 Northern Ireland and Sweden compared

	Northern Ireland	Sweden
Population	1 685 267	8 800 000
Area	14 121 km²	449 793km²
Population density	119 people/km²	19.6 people/km²

- Figure 10.6 shows that population density is highest in the southern regions of Scania and the Central Lowlands. It is in these regions that the largest centres of population are found including Gothenburg, Malmo and the capital Stockholm. These three cities account for 40 per cent of the total population of the country.

- The Norrland region, which covers two-thirds of Sweden, experiences winter conditions for seven months of the year due to its northerly latitude. This harsh climate combined with mountainous terrain presents formidable barriers to human settlement. The exploitation of forests and iron ore have led to the creation of a number of settlements including Lulea on the north-east coast where the iron ore is processed.

- The flat land and warmer climate which dominate the southern regions have proved more favourable for settlement. This area is served by a good road and rail network and the ports of Gothenburg, Malmo and Stockholm are ice-free all year round.

- Employment in both manufacturing (e.g. Volvo and Saab car assembly plants) and the service sector is concentrated in the major cities of the south.

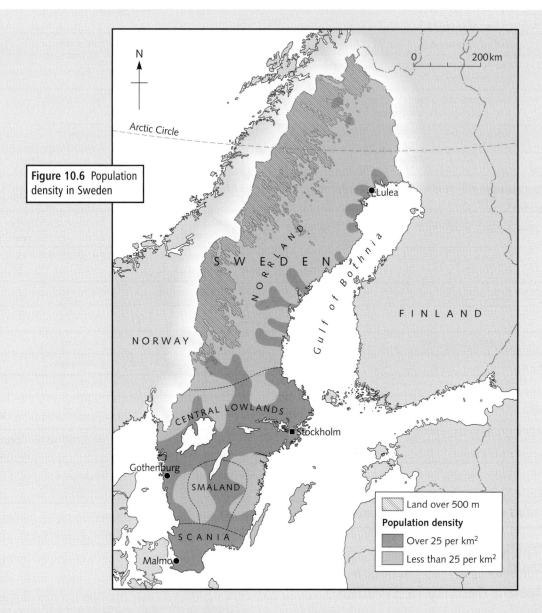

Figure 10.6 Population density in Sweden

Legend:
Land over 500 m

Population density
Over 25 per km²
Less than 25 per km²

Map labels: N, 0 200km, Arctic Circle, SWEDEN, NORRLAND, Lulea, Gulf of Bothnia, FINLAND, NORWAY, CENTRAL LOWLANDS, Stockholm, Gothenburg, SMALAND, SCANIA, Malmo

- The one exception to the north–south contrast in population density is Smaland. This is an area of wooded highland with poor soils. While lower than the surrounding areas of Scania and the Central Lowlands, its population density is still much higher than in the Norrland region.

Using your case study

Use this case study to answer questions on population distribution and density in an EU country. You need to know the regional variations and be able to explain the reasons for these variations.

Update

Go to *The NWW Coursemates* website for a link to 'sna' and click on 'English' (language) for a range of thematic maps and facts on Sweden.

Learn it!

1 a) Which parts of Sweden have the highest population density?

   b) What physical and economic factors explain this pattern?

2 What employment opportunities exist in Norrland?

1 State the meaning of the term *population distribution*. (2 marks)

2 Name one region of low population density and one region of high population density. (2 marks)

3 State two physical factors which help to explain the uneven nature of population density at the global scale. (6 marks)

EXAM TIPS

Make sure that you are able to name and locate at least two areas of high and low population density from a world map, and state relevant reasons for these, as this is a requirement of the CCEA specification – see question 2.

Back to ...

Back to *The NWW Coursemates* website to check your answers to the exam practice question.

11
Population change

➡ *The New Wider World*, pp 6–17, 22–31

KEY IDEAS

1 Changes in birth rates and death rates determine the size of the world population.

2 Rates of population growth vary over space and time.

3 Population pyramids reflect levels of development.

4 Population change can bring problems for LEDCs and MEDCs.

5 International migration can have positive and negative impacts.

Key words to know

Population change
Birth rate
Death rate

Figure 11.1 World population growth: 0 to 1800

Year	Population (in billions)
0	0.30
1000	0.31
1250	0.40
1500	0.50
1750	0.79
1800	0.98

Check this!...

1 How are birth rates and death rates measured?

2 Describe what is meant by the term 'population explosion'.

---

1 Changes in birth rates and death rates determine the size of the world population

Global **population change** depends upon the balance between the **birth rate** and the **death rate**. Migration does not influence global population size.

The birth rate is the average number of live births in a year for every 1000 people in the total population. The death rate is the average number of deaths per 1000 people in the population. The difference between the birth rate and the death rate is either the natural increase (where the birth rate is the higher) or the natural decrease (where the death rate is the higher). The natural increase is expressed as the percentage growth per year. To calculate natural increase use the following formula:

$$\text{Natural increase (\%)} = \frac{\text{birth rate (per 1000)} - \text{death rate (per 1000)}}{10}$$

For example, for Northern Ireland in 2001:

$$\frac{13.03 - 8.61}{10} = 0.44\%$$

Population growth

Up until the beginning of the nineteenth century the global population grew very slowly (Figure 11.1) as there was little difference between the birth and death rates.

For the next century and a half it grew at an increasingly faster rate, a process that has been referred to as a population explosion. During the 1960s and 1970s the world's population grew, on average, by a record 2 per cent per year (Figure 11.2). Estimates made at that time suggested that the world's population of 3039 million in 1960 would reach 7600 million by the end of the century and 11 000 million by 2050.

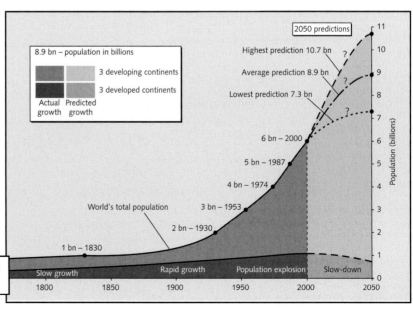

Figure 11.2 World population growth since 1800

2 Rates of population growth vary over space and time

The contrasting growth rates displayed in Figure 11.3 result in the developing countries adding 80 million people per year to the world's population compared with a figure of 1 million per year for the developed countries. Figure 11.3 shows:

- The continents with the fastest growth in population are the three developing ones of Africa, Asia and Latin America. Africa has the most rapid growth despite its high death rate caused by AIDS, crop failure and civil war.
- The continents with the slowest growth rate are the three developed ones of Europe, North America and Australasia (Oceania). Europe is the only continent showing a natural decrease, largely due to the impact of Eastern European countries.

The influence of migration on population change

Population change depends mainly upon the balance between the birth rate and the death rate. It is also, but to a lesser extent, affected by **migration** (Figure 11.4). Migration refers to the movement of people.

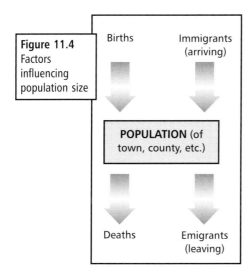

Figure 11.4
Factors influencing population size

Births   Immigrants (arriving)

POPULATION (of town, county, etc.)

Deaths   Emigrants (leaving)

	Average growth rate (%)	
	1980–90	2003
Developing countries	2.6	1.6
Africa		2.4
Asia		1.3
Latin America		1.7
Developed countries	0.9	0.1
Europe and former USSR		−0.2
North America		0.5
Oceania		1.1

Figure 11.3 Population growth in developed and developing countries

The demographic transition model

The **demographic transition model** (Figure 11.5) is an attempt to show how population changes (undergoes transition) over time. The word 'demographic' comes from demography, which is the study of population, and to undergo transition is to change. Like all models this is an attempt to simplify the complex situations found in the real world in order to make them easier to explain or understand.

The model, which was based on population changes in several industrialised countries in western Europe and North America, suggests that there are four stages through which all countries will eventually pass. The UK, being one of the world's first industrialised countries, has passed through all four stages.

Check this!...

1 Using Figure 11.3, describe the patterns of natural increase in developed and developing countries.

2 What does the figure for Europe and the former USSR in 2003 indicate about the balance between birth and death rates?

Key words to know

Migration
Demographic transition model

Back to …

The New Wider World **p11**
Figures 1.12 and 1.13 for
more details on contrasting
growth rates between the
developed and developing
continents.

The New Wider World **p13** for
information about China's
one-child policy.

Limitations of the demographic transition model

Like all models, the demographic transition model has certain
weaknesses. It assumed that all countries would follow the pattern of
the MEDCs in that population change would be stimulated by
industrialisation. While it is generally true that the MEDCs have
reached stage 4, it is now widely accepted that many of the LEDCs will
never become industrialised. Although the more developed LEDCs
have indeed reached stage 3, most of those that are the least developed
remain at stage 2 (Figure 11.5).

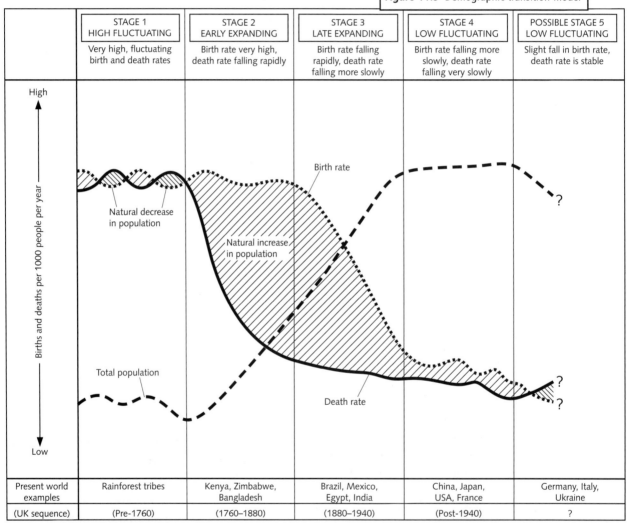

Figure 11.5 Demographic transition model

	STAGE 1 HIGH FLUCTUATING	STAGE 2 EARLY EXPANDING	STAGE 3 LATE EXPANDING	STAGE 4 LOW FLUCTUATING	POSSIBLE STAGE 5 LOW FLUCTUATING
	Very high, fluctuating birth and death rates	Birth rate very high, death rate falling rapidly	Birth rate falling rapidly, death rate falling more slowly	Birth rate falling more slowly, death rate falling very slowly	Slight fall in birth rate, death rate is stable
Present world examples	Rainforest tribes	Kenya, Zimbabwe, Bangladesh	Brazil, Mexico, Egypt, India	China, Japan, USA, France	Germany, Italy, Ukraine
(UK sequence)	(Pre-1760)	(1760–1880)	(1880–1940)	(Post-1940)	?

Year	Birth rate	Death rate
1926	22	15
1937	20	15
1951	21	13
1961	22	11
1971	21	11
1981	18	11
1991	17	10
2001	13	9

Figure 11.6 Birth and death rates
(per 1000) in Northern Ireland,
1926–2001

Since the 1990s it has been noticed that several MEDCs appear to be
entering a new, fifth stage. This stage, not shown in the original model,
is where the birth rate is beginning to fall below the death rate. It is
predicted that, should this trend continue, countries entering this stage
will eventually see a decrease in their total population.

Population changes in Northern Ireland

Figure 11.6 shows the changes in birth and death rates over the past
century. It is interesting to note the rapid decline in birth rates since
1971, while death rates have declined much more slowly.

1 Use Figure 11.5 to describe the changes in the birth and death rates across the five stages of the demographic transition model.

2 The death rate, even in an MEDC, rarely falls below 3 or 4 per 1000. Why is this?

3 Population pyramids reflect levels of development

Key words to know

Life expectancy
Population structure
Population pyramid

The rate of natural increase, the birth rate, the death rate and **life expectancy** all affect the **population structure** of a country. Life expectancy is the number of years that the average person born in a country can expect to live. The population structure can be shown by a **population pyramid** or, as it is sometimes known, an age–sex pyramid.

A population pyramid shows:
- the total population divided into five-year age groups, e.g. 5 to 9 years, 10 to 14 years
- the percentage of the total population, subdivided into males and females, in each of those groups
- the impact of migration.

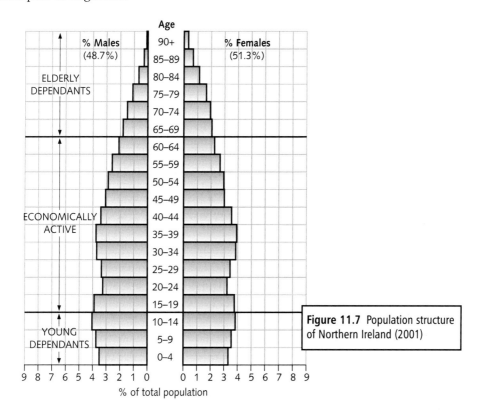

Figure 11.7 Population structure of Northern Ireland (2001)

The population pyramid for Northern Ireland (Figure 11.7) shows:
- a 'rectangular' shape indicating approximately the same number in each age group, a low death rate and a steady, or even a static, population growth
- a narrow base indicating a low and falling birth rate
- that more boys are born than girls (a higher percentage of boys aged under 4 years)
- relatively large numbers aged 65 years and over, indicating a long life expectancy
- that more females than males live to over 65 years

- a relatively large proportion of the population in the pre- and post-reproductive age groups and a relatively small number in the 15–64 age group, which is the one that produces children and most of the national wealth.

This last feature can be shown as the dependency ratio, i.e.

$$\frac{\text{Non-economically active, i.e. children (0–14) and elderly (65+)}}{\text{Economically active, i.e. those of working age (15–64)}} \times 100$$

For example, for Northern Ireland in 2001 (figures in millions):

$$\frac{0.370952 + 0.223325}{1.090990} \times 100 = \text{dependency ratio of 54.47}$$

This means that for every 100 people of working age, there were 54.47 people dependent upon them. This is slightly above the figure of 53.33 for the whole of the UK.

Most developed countries have a dependency ratio of between 50 and 70, whereas in developing countries the ratio is often over 100 due to the large numbers of children.

Population pyramids enable comparisons to be made between countries, and can help a country to plan for future service needs, such as old people's homes, if it has an ageing population, or fewer schools if it has a declining, younger population. Unlike the demographic transition model, population pyramids are influenced by migration. The influence of migration is usually observed in the economically active age groups.

Stages of development

Population pyramids are a useful measure of development as they display changes in the birth rates, death rates and life expectancy. The following case studies of Kenya and Italy illustrate how population structure can vary over time and between countries.

Check this!...

1 What information can be obtained from a population pyramid?

2 Explain how population pyramids can be used to plan for the future.

Case Study Extra

Population change in Kenya (LEDC)

Back to...

The New Wider World **p9** Figure 1.9 for more detail on Kenya's population structure.

1960	8 332 000
1970	11 498 000
1980	16 632 000
1990	24 032 000
2000	30 700 000

Figure 11.8 Kenya's growing population

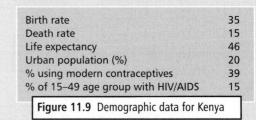

Birth rate	35
Death rate	15
Life expectancy	46
Urban population (%)	20
% using modern contraceptives	39
% of 15–49 age group with HIV/AIDS	15

Figure 11.9 Demographic data for Kenya

Kenya's population has grown rapidly in recent decades (Figure 11.8) and in the mid-1980s it had one of the highest growth rates in the world. This growth has been fuelled by a falling death rate as a result of:

- improved health care and hygiene levels
- greater access to clean drinking water and improved diet
- a younger population structure.

Figure 11.10 shows Kenya's changing population structure. The pyramids identify the high percentage of the population under 15 but the projection for 2025 indicates that the birth rate will have fallen substantially. This projected decline is closely linked to the increase in the percentage of Kenyans living in urban areas (Figure 11.9), because contraception is more widely available in urban areas and pressure on housing resources encourages couples to have a smaller family. A more sinister factor influencing birth and death rates is the threat of AIDS. Many women diagnosed with the HIV virus, which causes AIDS, do not want to have children due to the risk of passing on the disease, and those with full-blown AIDS have a much smaller chance of becoming pregnant. The increasing number with this disease has led to a rise in the death rate for the first time in over 100 years.

Using your case study

You can use this case study to answer questions on how the population size and structure of an LEDC (Kenya) has changed over time. Make sure you know how the population has changed, what has caused the falling death rate, and how the population is likely to change in the future.

Case study links

There is a link here to the growth of ecotourism (Chapter 9 pages 57–59). This sector provides employment for Kenya's growing population.

Update

Go to *The NWW Coursemates* website for the latest update of the population pyramid for Kenya.

Learn it!

1 Use Figure 11.8 to identify in which decade Kenya's population grew most rapidly.

2 How will changes in Kenya's population structure affect the dependency ratio?

3 Why are birth rates falling in Kenya?

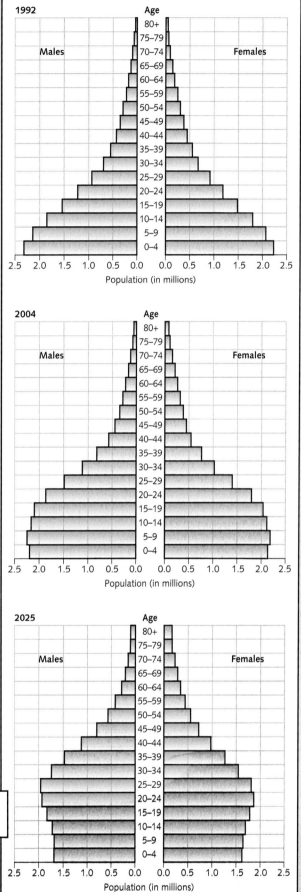

Figure 11.10 The changing population structure of Kenya

Population change in Italy (MEDC)

In contrast to Kenya, Italy's population has grown very slowly since 1960 (Figure 11.11). This has been caused by a low death rate and a falling birth rate. Italians enjoy a high standard of living and access to good medical care resulting in a long life expectancy (Figure 11.12) and a low death rate.

Figure 11.11 Population growth in Italy

1960	50 698 800
1970	53 685 301
1980	56 388 481
1990	56 694 360
2000	57 844 017

Figure 11.12 Demographic data for Italy

Birth rate	9
Death rate	10
Life expectancy	80
Urban population (%)	90
% using modern contraceptives	60
% of 15–49 age-group with HIV/AIDS	0.4

By 2003, the birth rate had fallen below the death rate. Italy's birth rate has been declining due to:

- a change in attitude towards children: increasingly couples view them as an economic burden rather than an asset
- the growth in the urban population: couples cannot afford to buy larger houses in the urban areas to accommodate a large family size
- a breakdown in the extended family: couples are often living far away from their families and have to take sole responsibility for child care
- the widespread availability and awareness of modern methods of contraception.

The population pyramids for Italy (Figure 11.13) demonstrate the impacts of a low birth rate and death rate. The 'greying' of the population – a phrase that refers to the increasing proportion of elderly people in a population – creates a number of serious questions which the Italian government will have to address. For example:

- Can the country afford to support an increasing number of elderly dependants?

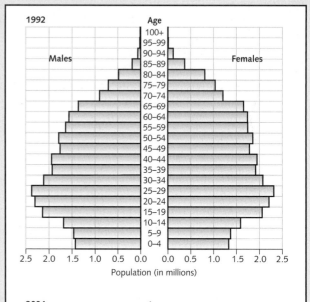
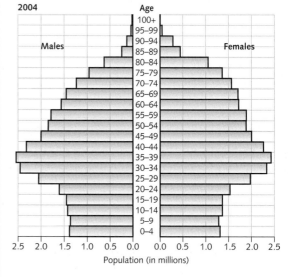
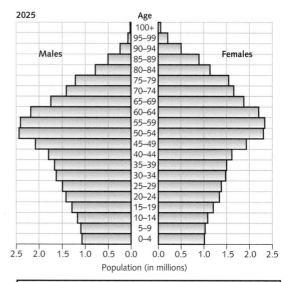

Figure 11.13 The changing population structure of Italy

- Will Italy's importance in the world be reduced by a shrinking population?
- Should labour shortages be met by encouraging immigration?

A possible solution has originated in Laviano, a small village south-east of Naples which is running so short of babies that in November 2003 its mayor announced the offer of £7000 to anyone who will have a baby and bring it up in the village.

Back to...

The New Wider World **p15** for information on Italy's ageing population.

Using your case study

You can use this case study to answer questions on how the population size and structure of an MEDC (Italy) has changed over time. Make sure you know how the population has changed, what has caused the falling birth rate, and how the population is likely to change in the future.

Update

Go to *The NWW Coursemates* website for the latest update of the population pyramid for Italy.

Learn it!

1 Use Figure 11.13 to describe Italy's changing population structure.

2 What problems arise from the changes in Italy's population?

4 Population change can bring problems for LEDCs and MEDCs

Key words to know

Youth dependency

Young people – a valuable resource?

Youth dependency occurs when a decline in the death rate is not matched by a decline in fertility levels. A high birth rate results in a high proportion of the population being under 15 years old. The percentage of the population under 15 for a selection of countries at different levels of development is shown in Figure 11.14.

In the case of Niger, half the population has yet to reach reproductive age so even if birth rates were to drop sharply in the short term, the population would still almost double in the coming years.

The high birth rates and large family size of many LEDCs can be attributed to a number of factors:

- Many children are needed to help work on the land, to carry wood and water, and to care for their older relatives.
- A high infant mortality rate means that many children die before their first birthday.
- Religious beliefs may forbid birth control.
- A lack of education, especially for women, has an effect on family planning.
- There is a lack of access to and insufficient money for the supply of contraceptives.
- A large family can enhance a family's reputation in the local community, especially for the husband.

Young people are essential to ensure the future existence of any society. However, until they are employed and start to earn their own living, they are dependants. In many LEDCs this high level of youth dependency is putting pressure on the resources available and undermining attempts to achieve economic development.

Country	Population under 15
UK	19%
Australia	20%
Niger	50%
Brazil	30%
Bangladesh	40%

Figure 11.14 Percentage of population under 15 in selected countries

Back to ...

The New Wider World **p14**
Figure 1.17 for changes in
life expectancies for a
selection of countries.

The New Wider World **p15**
for information on the
ageing populations of Italy
and China.

Key words to know

Aged dependency

Country	% of population over 65
Italy	19
Japan	19
Sweden	17
UK	16
USA	13

Figure 11.15 The percentage of the population over 65 in selected countries

- At present, the large youthful population needs child-health care and education – two services that these countries cannot afford.
- In the future, there will be more people reaching child-bearing age. The West African country of Niger has a dependency ratio of 108 – of which 104 are youth dependants, a situation that has locked the country into a cycle of poverty. Therefore, although children are essential to the survival of a country, too many children can have an adverse effect on the quality of life and future economic development.

The growth of 'grey power'

There has been, initially in the more economically developed countries but also more recently in some of the less economically developed countries, an increase in life expectancy.

This, together with a falling birth rate, means that an increasingly higher proportion of a country's population live beyond 65, and even beyond 80. This process is referred to as ageing. By 2000, several of the most economically developed countries (mainly Japan and several in western Europe) had over 16 per cent of their population aged over 65 (Figure 11.15).

As the proportion of elderly people rises, these countries will experience an increasing level of **aged dependency**: there is a greater demand for services such as pensions, medical care and residential homes which will have to be paid for by a smaller proportion of people of working age.

An ageing population may put financial pressure on the economically active (i.e. the taxpayers) but they can also make a valuable contribution to society (Figure 11.16). The term 'grey power' has been used to describe the growing political, social and economic importance of this age group.

Figure 11.16 The problems and benefits of an ageing population

Problems	Benefits
• An increasing amount of money is needed for residential homes and sheltered accommodation; health care (e.g. home visits and free prescriptions); and social services (e.g. home help and providing meals). • An increasing amount of the family doctor's financial budget and time is taken up by the elderly. • Less money is available for younger age groups, e.g. for education, improvements in transport or the provision of leisure and social amenities. • There is an increase in long-term illnesses and those that make people house-bound, such as Parkinson's disease and Alzheimer's disease. • Families may have to spend more time caring for elderly relatives.	• Falling crime rates – as elderly people are less likely to be involved in criminal activity. • Increased demand for services and goods designed for the elderly creates employment. • Contributions to society, e.g. the elderly have the time to undertake important voluntary work and help in the care of children for working parents.

Check this!...

1 Why do LEDCs tend to experience higher rates of youth dependency?

2 Why does the UK have an ageing population?

3 What economic problems are caused by an ageing population?

5 International migration can have positive and negative impacts

What is migration?

Migration is a movement and in human terms usually means a change of home. However, as seen in Figure 11.17, it can be applied to temporary, seasonal and daily movements as well as to permanent changes both between countries and within a country.

- Permanent international migration is the movement of people between countries.
- Emigrants are people who leave a country.
- **Immigrants** are those who arrive in a country.
- The migration balance is the difference between the numbers of emigrants and immigrants.

Key words to know

Immigrant

	External (international)	**Between countries**
Permanent	i) Voluntary	West Indians to Britain
	ii) Forced (refugees)	Negro slaves to America, Kurds, Rwandans
	Internal	**Within a country**
	i) Rural depopulation	Most developing countries
	ii) Urban depopulation	British conurbations
	iii) Regional	North-west to south-east of Britain
Semi-permanent	For several years	Migrant workers (Portuguese factory workers into Dungannon)
Seasonal	For several months or several weeks	Mexican harvesters in California, holiday-makers, university students
Daily	Commuters	Belfast

Figure 11.17 Types of migration

International migration can be divided into two types – voluntary and forced.

- **Voluntary migration** is the free movement of migrants looking for an improved quality of life and personal freedom. For example:
  - employment, either to find a job, to earn a higher salary or to avoid paying tax
  - better climate, especially on retirement
  - social amenities such as hospitals, schools and entertainment.
- **Forced migration** is when the migrant has no personal choice but has to move due to natural disaster or to economic or social imposition. For example:
  - wars, creating large numbers of refugees
  - racial discrimination
  - natural disasters caused by floods, drought, earthquakes, volcanic eruptions or hurricanes
  - overpopulation, when the number of people living in an area exceeds the resources available to them.

Back to ...

The New Wider World **p22**
Figure 2.3 for a map
showing major international
migrations since 1945.

The impacts of migration

Northern Ireland has experienced both the positive and negative sides of migration since its formation in 1921. The so-called 'brain-drain' of young talent to mainland Britain and beyond has had an adverse effect on local communities and economic growth. Figures show that Northern Ireland experienced a net migration loss of 8800 in 1981, but by 2002 the trend had reversed, with a net migration gain of 100.

A positive aspect of migration in the Northern Ireland context has been the arrival of skilled immigrants to work in the health services. In recent years there has been a dramatic increase in the number of overseas nurses working in the 12 health trusts, with the number reaching 560 in 2003. This overseas workforce is mainly Filipino but there are others from Australia and India.

Another beneficiary of immigration are some of the food processing companies in Portadown and Dungannon which have used over a thousand migrant workers from Portugal in their factories as they are paid less than local workers.

Case Study

Turkish migrants to Germany

Back to...

The New Wider World **pp28–29** for the case study of Turkish migrants into West Germany 1945–89.

Using your case study

This case study illustrates both the negative (disadvantages) and positive (advantages) impacts of migration for the area of origin (Turkey) and the destination (West Germany). Use this case study to answer questions on international migration. Ensure that you can identify examples of both negative and positive impacts on both Turkey and West Germany.

Case study links

The population pyramid (Figure 2.18 on p28 of *The New Wider World*) illustrates how migration is selective by age and gender.

Germany is an example of a multicultural society (see the next section).

Learn it!

1 Why did the Turks migrate to Germany?

2 Identify two advantages and two disadvantages for the recipient country (Germany).

3 Why has the pressure on the Turkish community in Germany increased since 1989?

Back to ...

The New Wider World **pp30–31** for a further case study on migration, 'Immigrants into California', which focuses on Mexican workers migrating to California.

Multicultural societies

International migration creates multicultural societies – that is, societies composed of people of different nationalities, races, religions, languages and cultures. The UK is an example of a multicultural society (Figure 11.18).

Group	% in UK
White	92.0
Mixed	1.2
Indian	1.8
Pakistani	1.3
Bangladeshi	0.5
Other Asian	0.4
Black	2.0
Chinese	0.4
Other	0.4

Figure 11.18
Ethnic composition of the UK, 2001

A small proportion of immigrants have come from the Old Commonwealth (Australia, New Zealand and Canada) and are descendants of earlier British migrants to those countries. The largest proportion are New Commonwealth immigrants from former British colonies in the Indian subcontinent (India, Pakistan and Bangladesh), Africa (Nigeria) and the West Indies (Jamaica). This group, who are mainly non-white, migrated here because:

- Britain had a labour shortage after the Second World War. Many West Indians came here partly due to the 'push' factor of overcrowding in their own islands, but mainly due to the 'pull' of jobs in Britain. The British government actively encouraged people to apply for specific jobs, for example with London Transport. Unfortunately, many immigrants were underskilled and were forced to take poorly-paid jobs.
- Groups of Asians, including Hindus, Muslims and Sikhs, found themselves as religious or political refugees following the division of India. They came to Britain in the 1950s.

This ethnic diversity has brought many benefits but there are also problems (Figure 11.19). Racial violence and rioting has been most common in those areas where there are higher concentrations of ethnic minorities (London, the West and East Midlands and West Yorkshire). Northern Ireland has not escaped – a report from the Equality Commission in 2003 revealed that the incidence of racist attacks in Northern Ireland is higher, at 16.4 per 1000 of the population, than in England and Wales, where attacks are 12.6 per 1000.

Back to ...

The New Wider World **p24**
Figure 2.7 – a map of the location of ethnic minorities across the UK.

Challenges	Opportunities
• Residential segregation – immigrants may live together either for protection or for services unique to that community (e.g. place of worship). • Lack of understanding – tension can be created through a fear of the unknown. This is intensified by language differences. • Intimidation – ethnic minorities can be targeted and forced to leave their home. In 2003, the Housing Executive in Northern Ireland had to move 30 ethnic minority families due to attacks. • Race riots – recent summers have seen rioting breaking out between gangs of white and Asian youths in Oldham and Burnley in the north of England.	• Employment – ethnic minority workers help fill skills shortages in the UK. • Sport – many members make a valuable contribution to sport in the UK, e.g. Denise Lewis (athletics) and Sol Campbell (football). • Cuisine – ethnic groups introduce new food choices, e.g. Indian and Chinese restaurants are popular across the UK. • Culture – ethnic groups introduce new festivals, e.g. the 9000-strong Chinese community in Northern Ireland celebrate the Chinese New Year at the end of January with a number of special events. The 2004 celebrations were held at the Armagh Planetarium to mark China's entry into the space race. • Economic – the London Development Agency estimates that the Notting Hill Carnival in London (which began as a celebration of West Indian culture) brings in £93 million to the city's economy. • Music and television – the singer Craig David (R 'n' B music) and Sanjeev Bhaskar, star of the BBC programme 'The Kumars at No. 42', are just two of many talents which come from the minority ethnic population.

Figure 11.19 Challenges and opportunities of multiculturalism in the UK

Check this!...

1 What is a multicultural society?

2 Why do ethnic minorities tend to be geographically concentrated?

3 Describe two opportunities that may arise from a multicultural society.

EXAM PRACTICE

1 With reference to Figure 11.5, explain why a fifth stage has been added to the demographic transition model. (3 marks)

2 Describe and explain changes in the population structure for a named MEDC that you have studied. (7 marks)

3 The UK is an example of a multicultural society. Describe two of the challenges which may occur in multicultural societies. (4 marks)

Back to ...

The NWW Coursemates website to check your answers to the exam practice question.

EXAM TIPS

When answering questions on population structure, e.g. question 2, you may wish to draw rough sketches of population pyramids to illustrate the changes over time. However, in order to gain marks for doing so, you must ensure that you make reference to any sketches in your written answer.

12 Population and resources

1 Overpopulation is caused by an imbalance between population and resources

What are resources?

Resources can be defined as features of the environment that are needed and used by people. The term usually refers to natural resources which occur in the air, in water or on the land. These resources include raw materials (minerals and fuels), climate, vegetation and soils. Sometimes the term is widened to include human resources such as labour, skills, machinery and capital (Figure 12.1).

Natural resources are commonly subdivided into two groups:
- **Non-renewable** resources are said to be **finite** or non-sustainable as their exploitation and use will eventually lead to their exhaustion, e.g. fossil fuels and minerals.
- **Renewable** resources can be:
  - a flow of nature so that, being continuous, they can be used over and over again, e.g. solar and geothermal energy, wind and water power
  - sustainable, which means they are renewable and self-generating if left to nature, e.g. clean water, trees, fish, wildlife, soils, ecosystems and landscapes.

KEY IDEAS

1. Overpopulation is caused by an imbalance between population and resources.
2. MEDCs and LEDCs display contrasting levels of resource consumption.
3. Exploitation and consumption of energy can have impacts upon people and the environment.
4. Renewable energy is a sustainable resource.

Key words to know

Resource
Non-renewable
Finite
Renewable
Overpopulation

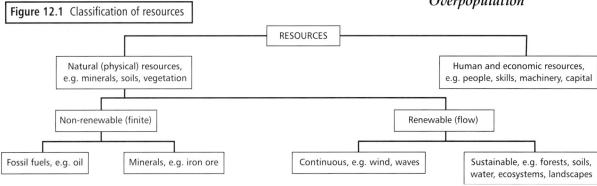

Figure 12.1 Classification of resources

RESOURCES

- Natural (physical) resources, e.g. minerals, soils, vegetation
  - Non-renewable (finite)
    - Fossil fuels, e.g. oil
    - Minerals, e.g. iron ore
  - Renewable (flow)
    - Continuous, e.g. wind, waves
    - Sustainable, e.g. forests, soils, water, ecosystems, landscapes
- Human and economic resources, e.g. people, skills, machinery, capital

Overpopulation

- **Overpopulation** occurs when there are too many people living in a country or region for the resources available. Under normal circumstances it means that there are likely to be insufficient jobs, houses, food and energy supplies to maintain a high standard of living.
- Bangladesh displays the characteristics of a country that is overpopulated, including having a high rate of unemployment (35 per cent). Although Bangladesh is densely populated (1018 people per km²), overpopulation is not caused by there being too many people, but rather too many people in relation to the resources available.
- In contrast, the tiny state of Singapore confirms this as it has a population density of 3972 people per km² but it is not overpopulated as it has the necessary resources to support its population.

- Canada is described as a country that experiences **underpopulation**. This situation arises when there are too few people in an area to make the maximum use of the resources available. In order to overcome this problem the Canadian government has encouraged large numbers of immigrants to settle in the country.

Overpopulation and underpopulation should not be confused with population density. Figure 12.2 shows that overpopulation and underpopulation are related to the population–resource balance rather than to population density.

Figure 12.2 The population–resource balance for selected countries

Status	High population density	Low population density
Overpopulation	Bangladesh	Ethiopia
Underpopulation	Netherlands	Canada

Causes of overpopulation

Four principle causes can be identified:
- population growth
- lack of resources
- low level of technology
- rise in consumption levels.

When considering the causes of overpopulation it is important to bear in mind that these factors have caused much debate amongst geographers over the last century. Some suggest that a large population is a symptom, not a cause, of overpopulation.

Impacts of overpopulation

If overpopulation occurs there will be a number of impacts on the local population:
- A decline in the standard of living, e.g. the daily calorie intake may fall if less food is available per head of the population.
- Increased pressure on resources – there will be increased levels of competition for food, jobs and housing.
- Outmigration will result if there are insufficient resources – millions left Ireland during the potato famines of the nineteenth century due to food shortages.

Achieving the balance

There are two possible responses to overpopulation in order to achieve a balance between the population of an area and the resources available:

1 Reduce the size of the population. This may occur by out-migration or by encouraging a decline in the birth rate through family planning initiatives. Such initiatives may be resisted if the population does not understand the reasons behind the scheme.
2 Use technology to develop or find new resources, e.g. reclaiming land from the sea or drilling for oil. However, this response may not be adopted due to a lack of money to develop or buy the necessary technology.

Achieving the balance between the population and the available resources is essential for the long-term well-being of the people but this delicate balance can be difficult to achieve for those countries trapped in a cycle of poverty.

Check this!...

1 Explain the difference between a finite resource and a renewable resource.

2 Why is Canada described as underpopulated?

3 Describe two impacts of overpopulation.

2 MEDCs and LEDCs display contrasting levels of resource consumption

Key words to know

Energy consumption

Figure 12.3 shows the **energy consumption** (how much energy per capita each country consumed) for the world in 2000. The map shows the gap between MEDCs and LEDCs. Although less than 25 per cent of the world's people live in the MEDCs, they consume two-thirds of the energy produced (the USA, with 5 per cent of the world's population, consumes 25 per cent).

% consumed		
	MEDCs	**LEDCs**
1990	75	25
2000	67	33
2010 (est)	62	38

Primary energy consumption expressed in kg of oil equivalent per person

- Over 10 000
- 2500–10 000
- 1000–2500
- 250–1000
- Under 250

Figure 12.3 World energy consumption, 2000

Reasons for the variation in world energy consumption

It is widely accepted that there is a link between the amount of energy consumed per capita in a country and that country's level of development. The more developed a country is, the more energy it needs for industry, transport and the home.

Since 1990 there has been a slow-down in the consumption of energy by most MEDCs, partly due to industrial decline and growing environmental concerns. There has also been an increase in consumption by many LEDCs with their growth in population and aspirations for a higher standard of living (Figure 12.3).

Back to ...

The New Wider World **p126** Figure 8.23 for a map showing world energy production levels.

The New Wider World **p127** for more information on energy consumption, and Figure 8.25 which shows sources and consumption of world energy in 2000.

Chapter 3 pages 15–16 for details on how the increasing consumption of non-renewable fossil fuels is contributing to global warming.

Check this!...

1   With reference to Figure 12.3, describe the pattern of world energy consumption.

2   Why do the poorest countries (e.g. Afghanistan) have such low levels of energy consumption?

3 Exploitation and consumption of energy can have impacts upon people and the environment

Key word to know

Exploitation

The **exploitation** of energy resources means that resources such as wood, coal and oil are used or developed to benefit people. Within the UK this process has brought wealth to the nation and to individual communities, e.g. Aberdeen has benefited greatly from the exploitation of North Sea oil. However, there have also been tragedies that have cost lives, e.g. in 1988 an explosion on the Piper Alpha oil platform in the North Sea killed 167 men. There is also the potential for environmental pollution, e.g. in 1993 the *Braer* oil tanker ran aground off the Shetland Islands and, as the ship broke up, the equivalent of 620 000 barrels of oil spilled into the sea killing over 1500 seabirds and several thousand salmon. However, a well-organised clean-up campaign helped to prevent long-term damage to the local environment.

The positive and negative effects of the exploitation of oil and gas which many MEDCs rely on are listed in Figure 12.4.

Back to ...

The New Wider World **p131** for the positive and negative impacts of oil exploration in Alaska.

Positive	Negative
Oil and gas can be used to meet the high energy demands (e.g. transport and electricity) of the MEDCs.	Oil and gas are subject to sudden international price changes and are vulnerable to political, economic and military pressure, e.g. the Gulf War (2003).
The extraction of oil and gas can create wealth and employment and may create a 'multiplier' effect through the demand for support services, e.g. Aberdeen.	Oil and gas are fossil fuels and therefore they do not represent a sustainable energy source. Predictions vary as to when these resources will run out but we know that they are a finite resource and will run out eventually.
Oil and gas are more efficient to burn than coal.	The extraction and transportation of oil can result in environmental disasters, e.g. *Exxon Valdez* (1989).
Oil and gas are easier to transport and distribute and less harmful to the environment than coal.	The consumption of oil and gas creates environmental problems at a range of scales, e.g. acid rain and global warming.

Figure 12.4 The positive and negative effects of the exploitation of oil and gas

Key words to know

Sustainable development

Back to ...

The New Wider World **p119** for further details on renewable energy sources.

The New Wider World **pp122–125** for details of a variety of renewable energy reserves: HEP, geothermal energy, wind power, solar energy, and power from hydrogen, tidal, waves and biomass sources.

4 Renewable energy is a sustainable resource

Using renewable sources of energy is considered to be a form of **sustainable development** as they are mainly forces of nature that can be used over and over again. The government target is that 10 per cent of all electricity is to be generated by renewable methods by 2010.

Lendrum's Bridge wind farm, County Tyrone

Back to...

The New Wider World **p124** Figure 8.17 for the location of wind farms in the UK.

Since 1994, Renewable Energy Systems has commissioned nine wind farms in Northern Ireland. These farms contribute to the 1.7 per cent of electricity in the province that is supplied by renewable resources.

The wind farm at Lendrum's Bridge (Figure 12.5) is situated midway between Fivemiletown and Fintona in County Tyrone on an area of high ground (over 300 metres).

Figure 12.5 Lendrum's Bridge wind farm

Phase 1 of the project comprising 9 turbines was completed in 1999. Eleven turbines representing phase 2 were added in 2002 bringing the total to 20, which can supply the electricity needs of 7000 homes. Figure 12.6 identifies the environmental impacts of the scheme.

The future development of wind farms in Northern Ireland is not assured. In November 2003 the Planning Service turned down an application to build an upland wind farm near Garrison in County Fermanagh due to the adverse impact that the development would have on the region's landscape and biodiversity resources. Plans for an offshore wind farm at Portstewart have been strongly opposed by local residents supported by golfer Darren Clarke and actor James Nesbitt.

Figure 12.6 Environmental impacts of wind farms

Positive environmental impacts
- Wind power is safe (no radioactive emissions) and clean (does not give off chemical emissions).
- Unlike fossil fuels, it does not contribute to global warming or acid rain.
- It has a minimal effect on local ecosystems. The wind farm covers only about 1% of the land on which it is sited, allowing the peatland habitats to survive around the turbines.

Negative environmental impacts
- Roadways and paths laid during construction of the wind farm had an impact on the drainage and habitats of this bogland area.
- The 30 metre tall turbines spoil the scenic attraction of Brougher Mountain on which they stand and can affect local bird life, e.g. the snipe and the curlew.
- The turbines generate noise pollution – between 40 and 50 decibels (a car engine generates 82 decibels).
- Wind does not blow all the time. At present electricity generated during storms cannot be stored for use during calm periods. Therefore the reliance on power stations will continue.

Using your case study

Use this Northern Ireland case study to answer questions on a renewable energy production scheme. You should be able to evaluate the benefits and problems to the environment and the potential for sustainable development.

Case study links

This case study has links with global warming covered in Chapter 3. The use of wind power reduces the levels of greenhouse gases, e.g. carbon dioxide, which cause global warming.

Update

Go to *The NWW Coursemates* website to find the link to Northern Ireland Energy. Follow the links from 'Community & Environment' to find out more about renewable energy in Northern Ireland. Also look for the link to 'res-ltd' for more details on wind farms in Northern Ireland.

Learn it!

1 Why have wind farms been created in Northern Ireland since 1994?

2 Describe one positive and one negative impact of this development on the environment.

3 Is this scheme a sustainable solution to Northern Ireland's energy needs? Explain your answer.

1 Name two examples of renewable resources. (2 marks)

2 Define the term *overpopulation*. (2 marks)

3 Explain why people living in the MEDCs consume two-thirds of the world's energy despite representing less than 25 per cent of the world's population. (4 marks)

4 Evaluate the environmental impacts of a named renewable energy scheme that you have studied. (8 marks)

Back to ...

The NWW Coursemates website to check your answers to the exam practice question.

EXAM TIPS

Make sure you always read the question carefully and focus on the key words. For example, in question 4 you are asked to 'Evaluate the environmental impacts of a named renewable energy scheme'. Stick to what the question asks, and do not be sidetracked into writing about economic issues, e.g. it is a cheap source of power.

⇨ *The New Wider World*, pp92, 136–143

13 Economic change in the UK

1 Economic change brings new uses for old buildings

Classification of economic activities

Economic activity can be divided into three main categories:
- **Primary** industries extract raw materials directly from the earth or sea. Examples include farming, fishing, forestry and mining.
- **Secondary** industries process and manufacture the primary products, e.g. steel making and furniture manufacture. They also include the construction industry and the assembly of component parts made by other secondary industries, e.g. car assembly.
- **Tertiary** industries provide a service. These include education, health, office work, retailing, transport and entertainment.

Since the 1980s a fourth group has been added:
- **Quaternary** industries provide **information services** and expertise. They include the relatively new micro-electronics industries.

Employment structure

The proportion of people working in each of the primary, secondary and tertiary sectors is called the employment structure.

The employment structure for Northern Ireland since 1851 for the three main groupings is shown in Figure 13.1. The decline in the primary sector can be largely attributed to the mechanisation of farming.

	% primary	% secondary	% tertiary
1851	58.7	30.5	10.8
1901	43.8	41.2	15.0
1951	28.3	35.7	36.0
1991	7.9	33.2	59.9
2003	3.0	20.0	77.0

Figure 13.1 The changing employment structure of Northern Ireland

Changes over time

The closure of Belfast's Harland and Wolff shipyard in 2003 is further evidence of the decline in manufacturing in Northern Ireland. The shipyard had been in existence since 1852. It employed over 35 000 workers at its peak but like other **traditional industries**, such as textiles and engineering, the shipyard could not compete with cheaper overseas competitors.

The decline in manufacturing has changed the urban landscape across Northern Ireland but the effects are seen most clearly in Belfast. Many old factories have been demolished but some industrial premises have undergone a change in function reflecting the changes in the economy.

KEY IDEAS

1 Economic change brings new uses for old buildings.

2 The location of high-tech industries is not restricted to traditional industrial areas.

Key words to know

Primary
Secondary
Tertiary
Quaternary
Information services
Traditional industries

From cigarette factory to cinema

When the Gallahers' cigarette factory opened in 1896 it was the largest in the world. At its peak the factory employed over 2000 workers, but this figure was halved by the time of its closure in 1988. The factory closed as a result of falling tobacco sales due to higher tobacco taxes and an increasing awareness of the health risks of smoking.

Figure 13.2 The Yorkgate complex

Following closure the factory was redeveloped as a shopping and leisure park at a cost of £35 million. The Yorkgate complex, which opened in 1991, is an ideal location for a retail and leisure park. Situated at the junction of the M2 motorway and the Westlink to the M1 motorway, it is easily accessible and has plenty of space for free parking. Part of the old red-brick factory was retained and modern purpose-built units were added. The complex includes a cinema, leisure centre, a bingo hall, several restaurants and a

wide range of shops. The advantages of this change of function to the local people and economy are shown in Figure 13.3.

Advantages to people	Economic advantages
• Creation of 400 jobs (part-time and full-time) • The redevelopment of this brownfield site has removed the eyesore of a derelict factory • Local people have benefited from the wide range of shops, services and entertainment venues	• The wages pump money into the local economy, creating a demand for more goods and services (multiplier effect). • Businesses pay rates that generate income for Belfast City Council. • The complex has attracted a small number of services, e.g. Iceland, onto adjacent sites.

Figure 13.3 Advantages of the Yorkgate complex

Using your case study

Use this case study as an example of a local or small-scale change in function of industrial premises. You should be aware of the new opportunities brought by this change in terms of the advantages to both people and the economy.

Learn it!

1 What locational advantages did the Gallahers' site offer for a shopping and leisure complex?

2 Describe the benefits of this change of function to the local people and the economy.

2 The location of high-tech industries is not restricted to traditional industrial areas

The growth of Britain's traditional industries in the nineteenth century (e.g. coal mining, shipbuilding and steel manufacture) was based on the use of coal, the development of technology to process local and imported raw materials, the creativity of the people and the ability to export manufactured goods. Consequently the major industrial areas were either on Britain's coalfields or in coastal ports located on deep-water estuaries.

The location, distribution and type of Britain's present-day manufacturing industry has changed considerably. Modern replacement industries, many of which are high-tech and connected with electronics, employ fewer people and are often located well away from the traditional manufacturing areas. They are said to be footloose as, not being tied to raw materials, they have a relatively free choice of location.

The term **high-technology** (or **high-tech**) **industry** refers, usually, to industries developed within the last 25 years and whose processing techniques often involve micro-electronics. Two possible subdivisions of high-tech industries are:

- the **sunrise industries** which have a high-technology base.
- **information technology** (IT) industries involving computers, telecommunications and micro-electronics.

As a highly skilled, inventive, intelligent workforce is essential, and as access to raw materials is relatively unimportant, these high-tech 'footloose' industries tend to become attracted to areas that the researchers and operators find attractive, from a climatic, scenic, health and social point of view. Within the UK such areas include:

- Silicon Glen in Central Scotland
- Sunrise Strip which follows the route of the M4 from London westwards towards Newbury, Bristol and into South Wales.

Key words to know

High-tech industry
Sunrise industry
Information technology

Case Study

The M4 Corridor (Sunrise Strip)

Back to...

The New Wider World **p140** for the case study of the M4 Corridor, a core region for high-tech industries in the UK.

Using your case study

This case study demonstrates factors that influence the location of high-tech industries. You should be aware of how this region meets the necessary criteria, e.g. good communications and proximity to a number of universities.

Update

Go to *The NWW Coursemates* website for a link to 'M4 Corridor' and follow the link entitled 'About the M4 corridor'. This provides details on places within the corridor and information on the IT companies operating in the area.

Learn it!

1 Describe the location of the M4 Corridor.

2 What economic advantages does this region offer to high-tech companies?

3 Why do high-tech companies tend to locate in, or near to, attractive environments?

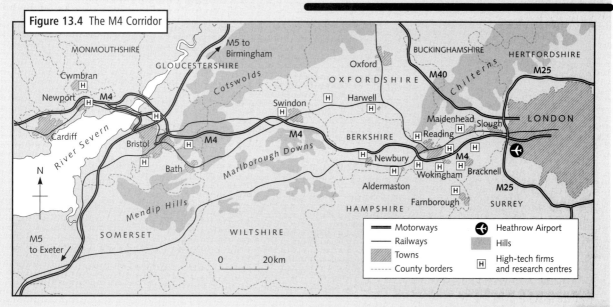

Figure 13.4 The M4 Corridor

1 Provide two examples of primary industries. (2 marks)

2 Define the term *tertiary industry*. (2 marks)

3 With reference to Figure 13.1, describe the changes in the employment structure in Northern Ireland since 1951. (2 marks)

4 State fully one reason for the decline of Northern Ireland's traditional industries. (2 marks)

5 For a named case study, describe two advantages brought about by a changeof function of industrial premises. (4 marks)

Back to ...

The NWW Coursemates website to check your answers to the exam practice question.

EXAM TIPS

Where a question asks you to refer to specific data, for example in question 3, make sure you quote information from the source to support your answer.

⇨ *The New Wider World*, pp144–145

14

The global economy

KEY IDEAS

1 A global shift has occurred in the location of manufacturing industry.

2 Transnational corporations create benefits and problems for LEDCS.

Key words to know

Transnational corporation (TNC)
Globalisation
Relocation
Locational advantage
Investment

1 A global shift has occurred in the location of manufacturing industry

A **transnational corporation (TNC)**, also referred to as a multinational company, is one that operates in many countries, regardless of national boundaries. The headquarters and main factory is usually in a more economically developed country with, increasingly, branch factories in less economically developed countries. One example in Northern Ireland is the American firm Fruit of the Loom which has a branch factory near Eglinton, County Londonderry. Transnationals are believed to directly employ some 40 million people around the world, to indirectly influence an even larger number, and to control over 75 per cent of world trade.

The relatively new term **globalisation** is used to describe those TNCs that see the world, rather than the local area, as their supplier of labour, raw materials and component parts and their areas of sales. The globalisation of manufacturing has been made possible by:

- falling transport costs, e.g. use of containers
- improvements in global communications (ICT)
- a gradual removal of barriers to world trade.

TNCs have created a world market for their products. Desmond's clothing company is an example of a TNC based in Northern Ireland which has embraced the concept of globalisation. The company's last manufacturing base in Northern Ireland closed in 2003 completing the **relocation** of production to cheaper overseas plants in Turkey, Sri Lanka and Bangladesh.

Car firms were amongst the first to opt for transnational operations. They found that moving to other parts of the world had **locational advantages**. For example, they could:

- get around trade barriers which may have been erected to protect home markets
- reduce costs by gaining access to cheaper labour and/or raw materials
- be nearer to large markets (centres of population).

Moving location has enabled TNCs to boost their profits by reducing costs or increasing sales.

2 Transnational corporations create benefits and problems for LEDCS

The governments of LEDCs welcome **investment** by TNCs – in some cases the TNCs may have a higher turnover than the GNP of the country in which it is investing (Figure 14.1). The investment represents a commitment of money, time and expertise by the TNC in order to make a profit.

Industrial corporation	Country	Sales ($ millions)	Employees	Country (examples)	GNP ($ millions per country, not per person)
1 General Motors	USA	133 622	710 800	Rwanda	1499
2 Ford Motor	USA	108 521	322 200	Afghanistan	3100
3 Exxon	USA	97 825	91 000	Nepal	3174
4 Royal Dutch/Shell group	UK/Netherlands	95 134	117 000	Ethiopia	5200
5 Toyota Motor	Japan	85 283	109 279	Kenya	6743
6 Hitachi	Japan	68 581	330 637	Ghana	7036
7 IBM (International Business Machines)	USA	62 716	267 196	Sri Lanka	10 688
8 Matsushita Electric Industrial	Japan	61 384	254 059	Bangladesh	25 882
9 General Electric	USA	60 823	222 000		
10 Daimler-Benz	Germany	59 102	366 736		
11 Mobil	USA	56 576	61 900		
12 Nissan Motor	Japan	53 760	143 310		
13 British Petroleum	UK	52 385	72 600		
14 Samsung	South Korea	51 345	191 303		

Figure 14.1 Dominance of transnational corporations

Key words to know

Infrastructure
Export

However, for the LEDCs it represents an opportunity for the creation of jobs and economic development. Investment by TNCs may also bring improvements in a country's **infrastructure**. The infrastructure is the basic network of services that businesses and communities rely on, e.g. road, rail and air links, and the supply of water and electricity. Good infrastructure is important to ensure the rapid import and **export** of goods and raw materials.

Check this!...

1 What is a TNC?

2 What are the economic benefits of globalisation?

3 Explain why a TNC may invest in the infrastructure of an LEDC.

Figure 14.2 Advantages and disadvantages of TNCs to LEDCs

	Advantages	Disadvantages
For people	• Brings work to the country and uses local labour • Local workforce receives a guaranteed income • Improves the levels of education and technical skill of the people • Improvements in infrastructure, e.g. roads, water supply	• Local labour force is usually poorly paid • Very few local skilled workers are employed – managers are brought in from MEDCs • Financial incentives given to TNCs to locate in the country possibly better spent on improving housing, diet and sanitation • Jobs are not secure as decisions are made outside the country, and the company can pull out at any time • There is insufficient attention to safety and health factors
For the environment	• People move to urban areas reducing pressures on rural areas, e.g. overcultivation, overgrazing	• Increased pollution levels in urban areas (e.g. air and water) as infrastructure cannot cope with growing population • TNCs may cause harmful pollution because environmental laws are not enforced, e.g. Unilever dumped mercury in Kodiakanal, India

Back to ...

The New Wider World
pp144–145 for information on Ford, another example of a TNC.

When evaluating the impact of TNCs on LEDCs it is important to remember that their goal is to maximise profit and although investment does bring many advantages for these countries, the economic development of LEDCs is not a priority for TNCs. Figure 14.2 outlines the advantages and disadvantages of TNCs to LEDCs.

Gap Inc. Clothing Company

Gap Inc. was founded in 1969 in California and has grown rapidly to employ 165 000 people working in, or supporting, more than 4200 stores throughout North America and Europe. Gap manufactures in 64 countries, of which 45 can be classified as LEDCs or NICs (newly industrialised countries).

The sourcing process

Gap selects manufacturers around the world – a process called sourcing – to manufacture their products. Sourcing enables Gap to take advantage of skills found in particular regions, e.g. Asian factories offer expertise in working with silk. This method of production also enables Gap to keep production costs low as the factories employ cheap labour. For example, Gap sources work to Saipan, one of the northern Marianas Islands in the Pacific, a US commonwealth that is exempt from American labour, immigration and customs laws. The wage there is $3.05 per hour – far less than the $5.15 per hour minimum wage in the USA and the $6.75 per hour rate in California.

Back to...

Figure 14.1 opposite for the advantages and disadvantages of TNCs to LEDCs.

Gap's code of conduct

The manufacture of Gap clothing creates much needed employment in a large number of LEDCs, but the company has faced pressure from human rights groups over its working conditions (12–16 hour shifts with no overtime pay) and low wages (in some cases $1/day) in the factories.

As Gap does not own the factories that produce its clothing range, it does not have full control over what happens within the factories. Where there is evidence of human rights abuses or illegal pollution of the environment the company has been seen to act quickly to protect its name. In 1999, a BBC team discovered the use of child labour in factories producing clothing for Gap in Thailand and as a result the order was immediately suspended.

Gap now employs more than 90 full-time employees around the world who are dedicated to implementing a set of rules for all their suppliers which should help to improve the lives of garment workers. Factories not conforming to the standards have their orders cancelled. However, as these factories are independent of Gap and may be producing garments for a range of producers, it can be difficult for Gap to enforce its own rules.

Anti-globalisation campaign groups have targeted Gap along with other TNCs, for exploiting the world's poor (Figure 14.3).

Using your case study

It is also important to understand that the relocation of Gap production to LEDCs brings advantages and disadvantages to the countries concerned.

Update

Go to *The NWW Coursemates* website for a link to Gap Inc. Click on 'about gap inc.' to find out how the company is run, including how it sources its products.

Another link to 'Clean Clothes' includes the Gap symbol which will take you to the latest news on working conditions in factories supplying Gap.

Learn it!

1 Give two examples of places where Gap manufactures its products.

2 Why does Gap select manufacturers from around the globe to make its clothes?

3 Describe the problems that workers may encounter in the Gap supply factories.

1 Define the term *globalisation*. (2 marks)

2 a Name a TNC that you have studied. (1 mark)

   b State fully two reasons why this TNC manufactures in LEDCs. (6 marks)

3 Identify one advantage and one disadvantage of TNCs locating in LEDCs. (4 marks)

Back to ...

The NWW Coursemates website to check your answers to the exam practice question.

EXAM TIPS

Do not spend too long on each question. Remember that each of the six themes in the Specification is examined by a 40 mark question. You should spend 30 minutes per theme, which works out at less than a minute per mark, e.g. for question 3 you should spend no more than 3 minutes.

15 Sustainable development

1 A development gap exists between MEDCs and LEDCs

The simplest and most commonly used map to show differences in development is shown in Figure 15.1. Here, the world is divided into two groups:

- The more economically developed countries (MEDCs) which include the richer, more industrialised countries of the so-called developed 'North'.
- The less economically developed countries (LEDCs) which include the poorer, less industrialised countries of the so-called developing 'South' or 'Third World'.

KEY IDEAS

1 A development gap exists between MEDCs and LEDCs.

2 Appropriate technology can encourage sustainable economic development.

3 Global trading partners are interdependent.

4 Fairtrade offers advantages to LEDCs and MEDCs.

5 Aid can have positive and negative outcomes.

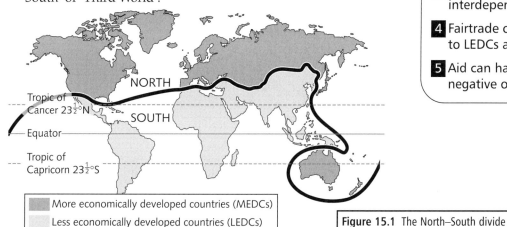

More economically developed countries (MEDCs)
Less economically developed countries (LEDCs)

Figure 15.1 The North–South divide

Like any classification, the division of the world in this way creates problems, as there may be large differences *between* countries within each grouping. The figures for the LEDCs in particular as listed in Figure 15.2 demonstrate this problem. It is also important to note that there may be contrasts in development levels *within* a country.

Development indicators

Geographers have suggested several methods by which they can measure development.

Economic wealth

The wealth of a country is measured by its gross national product per capita, i.e. its GNP per person. The GNP per person is the total value of goods and services produced by a country in a year, divided by the total number of people living in that country. To make comparisons between countries easier, GNP is given in US dollars (US$).

GNP values are relatively simple to calculate but they should be used with caution as the values:

- do not show differences in wealth between people and places in a country
- can underestimate the wealth of LEDCs as the informal sector that plays a major role in their economies is not included
- do not take account of currency fluctuations – the purchasing power of one American dollar varies from country to country.

Back to …

The New Wider World **p180**
Figure 11.2 for a map showing world GNP.

Social indicators

Although to people living in a Western society economic development often means a growth in wealth, other indicators have also been suggested. Figure 15.2 shows possible links between development and a range of social measures.

Figure 15.2 Indicators of development

| | Country | Economic wealth | Social indicators | | | | | | Other indicators | | | |
| | | | Population | | | Health | | | Literacy | Nutrition | Employment | Energy consumption |
	Country	GNP per capita (US$)	Birth rate*	Death rate*	Natural increase*	Infant mortality	Life expectancy	Population per doctor	% adult literacy	Calories per person per day	% in agriculture	Tonnes coal equivalent per year
MEDCs	Japan	39 640	9	8	1	4	81	600	99	2932	7	4.74
	USA	26 980	15	9	6	7	77	420	99	3699	3	10.74
	Italy	19 020	9	10	−1	6	79	211	98	3507	9	4.02
	UK	18 700	12	11	1	6	77	300	99	3276	2	5.40
Middle-income LEDCs (NICS)	Malaysia	3 890	25	4	21	8	73	2 564	87	2977	27	1.80
	Brazil	3 640	22	7	15	34	68	1 000	84	2974	25	0.44
	Mexico	3 320	24	5	21	27	75	621	91	3097	28	1.89
Low-income LEDCs	India	340	26	9	17	70	61	2 439	85	2496	64	0.35
	Kenya	280	34	14	20	76	48	10 000	80	1976	80	0.11
	Bangladesh	240	28	8	20	58	59	12 500	60	2085	65	0.08
	Ethiopia	100	44	15	29	118	52	33 000	64	1858	86	0.03

* Birth rates, death rates and natural increase are measured per 1000

← **Back to ...**

The New Wider World **p181** Figure 11.4 for further differences between MEDCs and LEDCs.

The New Wider World **pp182–183** for details on the Human Development Index (HDI), which the UN uses as its measure of development.

- **Population** – In general, the MEDCs have lower birth rates and a slower natural increase than the LEDCs. Population structures (Chapter 11) show that the MEDCs have a smaller proportion of children aged under 15 and a higher proportion of people aged over 65 than developing countries.
- **Health** – Similarly, MEDCs have a lower infant mortality rate, a longer life expectancy and fewer people per doctor than the LEDCs.

Other indicators

These include measures related to adult literacy, diet, employment structures and energy consumption (Figure 15.2). Notice, however, that many of these criteria are themselves related to the wealth of a country. For example, the wealthier and therefore more economically developed a country is, the more it can spend on health care, education, energy provision and providing other services. This suggests that a country has to increase its GNP if it is to improve the standard of living and quality of life of its inhabitants.

Check this!...

1 What does 'GNP per capita' measure?

2 For the UK and a low-income LEDC, describe the development differences for any three development indicators in Figure 15.2.

3 Suggest how adult literacy levels may be related to the GNP values.

2 Appropriate technology can encourage sustainable economic development

Appropriate technology

In most LEDCs, not only are high-tech industries too expensive to develop, they are usually inappropriate to the needs of the local people and to the environment in which they live. An **appropriate technology** is exactly what it says – a technology that is appropriate or suitable to the place in which it is used.

An appropriate technology can contribute to a more sustainable way of life for people who are rich or poor, living in places that may be developed or developing. If the place is developed and industrialised and its inhabitants are well-off, then the appropriate technology is more likely to be high-tech. If the place is underdeveloped and its inhabitants are poor, then alternative forms of technology could be adopted. These alternative forms may include:

- labour-intensive projects – to tackle high unemployment
- technology that is sustainable and fully utilises the existing skills of local people
- local crafts and industries using local natural resources and, where possible, recycling materials
- low-cost schemes using technologies that people can afford and manage.

Sustainable development

The use of appropriate technology can play a central role in ensuring that development is sustainable. **Sustainable development** should, according to the United Nations (UN): '... meet the needs of the present without compromising the ability of future generations to meet their own needs.' It should lead to an improvement in people's:

- quality of life – allowing them to become more content with their way of life and the environment in which they live
- standard of living – enabling them, and future generations, to become better off economically.

This may be achieved in a variety of ways:

- by encouraging economic development at a pace a country can afford and can manage to prevent the country falling into debt
- by developing technology that is appropriate to the skills, wealth and needs of local people and by developing local skills so that they may be handed down to future generations
- by using natural resources without harming the environment, developing materials that will use fewer resources, and using materials that will last longer.

Key words to know

Appropriate technology
Sustainable development

Back to ...

The New Wider World **pp150–151** for examples of appropriate technology projects in Nepal and Kenya.

The New Wider World **p184** Figure 11.8 for more about differences between sustainable development and non-sustainable development.

Check this!...

1 What is sustainable development?

2 How can the use of appropriate technology ensure that development is sustainable?

Sustainable development in Ladakh, India

A range of projects in Ladakh, India demonstrates that sustainable development can be achieved even in a difficult environment through the use of appropriate technology.

← **Back to...**

The New Wider World **p185** for the case study of Ladakh, India.

Set deep in the Indian Himalayas on the western edge of the Tibetan plateau, Ladakh, or 'Little Tibet', is one of the highest and driest inhabited places on Earth. Ladakh experienced Western-style development in the 1970s but the subsidised imports and promotion of a 'Western' lifestyle had a detrimental impact on the economy and society. Since the mid-1970s local people have been working with non-government organisations (NGOs) to encourage sustainable development through the application of appropriate forms of technology.

Using your case study
This is an example of a sustainable development project at a local scale in an LEDC which is using appropriate technology. You need to be able to identify how the project has encouraged economic and social development without harming the environment.

Case study links
The use of renewable energy in this project links to the sustainable approaches to energy use covered in Chapter 12 pages 82–83.

Update
Go to *The NWW Coursemates* website for a link to the International Society for Ecology and Culture for more details on the projects in Ladakh.

Learn it!

1 List the physical characteristics of this area.

2 Describe two sustainable development projects in this region.

3 Identify the social, economic and environmental benefits of these projects.

3 Global trading partners are interdependent

Key words to know

Trade
Interdependent
Trade deficit

No country is self-sufficient in the full range of raw materials (food, minerals and energy) and manufactured goods that are needed by its inhabitants. To try to obtain them, countries must trade with one another. **Trade** is the flow of commodities from producers to consumers, and it is important in the development of a country. Countries that trade with other countries are said to be **interdependent**.

- Raw materials, goods and services bought by a country are called imports.
- Those sold by a country are exports.
- The difference between a country's imports and exports is known as its trade balance.

One way for a country to improve its standard of living and to become more wealthy is to sell more goods than it buys. Unfortunately, if several countries export more than they import, then other countries will have to import more than they export. The result is that some countries have a trade surplus, allowing them to become richer, while others have a **trade deficit**, making them poorer and likely to fall into debt.

Patterns of world trade

There is a wide imbalance of trade between the LEDCs and the MEDCs. This is mainly because:

- the LEDCs provide primary goods such as foodstuffs and raw materials – primary goods are usually sold to the MEDCs at low and often fluctuating prices

- the MEDCs process primary goods, which they either possess themselves or obtain from LEDCs, into secondary (or manufactured) goods – secondary goods are sold at high and usually steady prices.

Although the prices of primary goods have increased over the years, the prices of secondary goods have increased far more rapidly. This means:

- The MEDCs that export manufactured goods earn increasingly more than the LEDCs which have only primary goods to sell. The result (with the exception of the newly industrialised countries, e.g. Taiwan) is a widening trade gap between the MEDCs and the LEDCs.
- Although 82 per cent of the world's population lived in LEDCs in 2000, the LEDCs contributed only 24 per cent to the world's trade. Over time, the MEDCs have steadily increased their share of world trade – a trend that seems likely to continue.

Problems of trade

The pattern of world trade creates a number of problems for the LEDCs, leaving them unable to achieve sustained economic development. This situation has been made worse through the desire of the MEDCs to control trade by imposing trade barriers which they hope will protect jobs and industries within their own country. These barriers can take two forms:

- Tariffs are taxes or customs duties paid on imports. Tariffs can increase the cost of imports (helping the trade balance) and thus protect home-made products.
- Quotas limit the amount of goods that can be imported. Quotas tend to be restricted to primary goods and so work against the LEDCs.

These trade barriers, in conjunction with the contrasting values of raw materials and manufactured goods, create a trade trap for the LEDCs (Figure 15.3).

Back to …

The New Wider World **pp186–187** Figures 11.10 and 11.12 for more information on international trade.

Figure 15.3 The trade trap

Check this!...

1 Define the term *interdependence*.

2 Why do many LEDCs have a large trade deficit?

3 With reference to Figure 15.4, state why these export figures put the named LEDCs in a dangerous economic position.

A further problem for many LEDCs, and especially those in Africa, is that they rely upon just one or two major commodities for export (Figure 15.4). The price paid for these commodities is often fixed by the MEDCs. If there is a world recession, an overproduction of a crop or mineral, a change or a fall in the demand for a product, a crop failure, or the exhaustion of a mineral, then the economy of the producing country can be seriously affected.

Country	Exports	Percentage of total exports
Kenya	Tea and coffee	54
Ghana	Cocoa	76
Honduras	Bananas	78
Zambia	Copper	86
Nigeria	Oil and gas	97

Figure 15.4 The over-reliance of selected LEDCs on a small range of exports

4 Fairtrade offers advantages to LEDCs and MEDCs

Countries at a global scale are interdependent. However, the economic power lies in the hands of the MEDCs. The idea of **fairtrade** is to redress this imbalance by putting farmers in the LEDCs into a stronger trading position. Farmers in the LEDCs have traditionally been in a vulnerable trading position due to:

- low and insecure prices for their products which keep them in poverty
- the threat of losing their land and home if there is a drop in prices
- a lack of knowledge of world markets or
- no means of processing or transporting their crop, which puts them in a weak negotiating position.

Fairtrade – benefiting the LEDCs

The Fairtrade trademark (Figure 15.5) states that Fairtrade 'guarantees a better deal for Third World Producers'. This is achieved by:

- guaranteeing a minimum price that covers the cost of production and provides a basic living wage
- providing low interest credit for producers so that they have the necessary resources to grow their crops
- encouraging long-term trading relationships between the farmers and buyers to ensure that farmers can plan for the future
- helping small landowners to join together to form co-operatives with a democratic, participative structure – these co-operatives can then sell large quantities of crops at a guaranteed price.

Fairtrade prices include a social premium for farmers and workers to invest in community projects. This investment has allowed producers to improve their homes, improve education and health care, build roads, invest in their businesses or diversify into other income-generating projects. In 2004 it was estimated that Fairtrade benefited 4.5 million producers (Figure 15.6) and their families across the world.

Fairtrade – advantages to the MEDCs

Fairtrade produce first came on the market in 1994 and as Figure 15.7 indicates, sales have grown rapidly since then. The first products carrying the Fairtrade mark were limited to tea, coffee and chocolate but by 2003 there were over 180 products marketed by over 80 companies.

Guarantees a **better deal** for Third World Producers

FAIRTRADE

Figure 15.5 The Fairtrade trademark

Figure 15.6 A farmer growing Fairtrade coffee in Costa Rica

Retail value (£ million)	1998	1999	2000	2001	2002
Coffee	13.7	15.0	15.5	18.6	23.1
Tea	2.0	4.5	5.1	5.9	7.2
Chocolate/cocoa products	1.0	2.3	3.6	6.0	7.0
Honey products	n/a	> 0.1	0.9	3.2	4.9
Bananas	n/a	n/a	7.8	14.6	17.3
Other	n/a	n/a	n/a	2.2	3.5
TOTAL	16.7	21.8	32.9	50.5	63.0

Figure 15.7 The growth in retail sales of Fairtrade produce

Between 2000 and 2002, Fairtrade sales increased in the UK by 90 per cent, making the UK the second largest market for Fairtrade products after Switzerland. Buying Fairtrade may cost more, but there are advantages to those living in the MEDCS:

- Farmers supplying companies using the Fairtrade mark have to meet strict environmental regulations. For example, banana growers have to recycle plastic waste – a small step but one that reduces pressure on global resources.
- Providing farmers in the LEDCs with a fair wage gives them greater spending power which could potentially boost export sales from the MEDCs.

5 Aid can have positive and negative outcomes

Many LEDCs have come to rely upon aid. **Aid** is the giving of resources by one country, or by an organisation (known as the donor), to another country (the recipient). The resource may be in the form of:

- money, although this may be given as a grant or a loan that has to be repaid
- goods, food, machinery or technology aimed at short-term relief or long-term benefit (Figure 15.8)
- people who have skills and knowledge, e.g. teachers, nurses and engineers.

The basic aim in giving aid is to help poorer countries develop their economy and services in order that they may improve their standard of living and quality of life.

Figure 15.8 identifies the five categories of aid, although on occasions these may overlap, for example in the provision of voluntary, short-term aid.

In reality, the giving of aid is often complex and controversial as it does not always benefit the country to which it is given (Figure 15.9).

Check this!...

1 Describe two benefits of Fairtrade to producers in the LEDCs.

2 With the aid of Figure 15.7, describe the changing demand for Fairtrade produce.

Key word to know

Aid

Back to ...

The New Wider World **p191** Figure 11.18 which shows the donors and recipients of aid.

Figure 15.8 Types of aid

Type of aid	Definition
Government (bilateral)	Given directly by a richer country (donor) to a poorer country (recipient) – often tied with 'strings attached'
International organisations (multilateral)	Given by organisations such as the World Bank and the IMF (International Monetary Fund)
Voluntary	Non-governmental organisations such as Tearfund and ActionAid which collect money and receive gifts for people in LEDCs
Short-term/emergency	Needed to cope with the effects of environmental hazards such as earthquakes and tropical storms. Immediate help may include food, clothes and temporary shelters
Long-term/Sustainable	Organisations such as Intermediate Technology Development Group that help people in LEDCs to support themselves

Figure 15.9 Problems with aid

Although the giving of aid can be problematic, it can represent the difference between life and death, especially when disaster strikes and there is a need for short-term aid, e.g. the Mozambique flood in 2000 or the Ethiopian famines of 1984 and 2002. Aid projects can also play an important role in the long-term development of LEDCs by:

- increasing self-sufficiency
- improving levels of health and education
- using small-scale appropriate technology.

Northern Ireland – an aid recipient

Aid is usually pictured as moving from MEDCs to LEDCs but aid can also move within the MEDCs in an attempt to reduce regional inequalities. Northern Ireland has benefited greatly from financial aid from the European Union due to its peripheral location within Europe, its high rates of unemployment and the impacts of 'the troubles'. This is an example of multilateral aid. Between 2000 and 2006 Northern

Ireland will receive £870 million from the various EU funds. This money covers a wide range of projects, for example:

- tourist development
- farm diversification
- transport infrastructure.

The Waterfront Hall in Belfast is one of many buildings which displays a plaque showing a blue flag with 12 gold stars, indicating EU funding. The level of funding is likely to fall after 2006 due to the increased levels of economic and political stability in the province and the greater needs of the new member states of eastern Europe.

Check this!...

1 What is aid?

2 Describe three ways in which aid may create problems for the recipient country.

3 Explain why Northern Ireland receives aid from the EU.

EXAM PRACTICE

1 Using Figure 15.2, give the value of a social and economic indicator of development for the UK. (2 marks)

2 Define the term *trade deficit*. (2 marks)

3 For your small-scale study of a sustainable development project, explain how it has contributed to the protection of the environment. (5 marks)

4 Describe in full two benefits of fairtrade to producers in LEDCs. (4 marks)

5 Suggest two examples of emergency or short-term aid. (2 marks)

EXAM TIPS

Where a question asks you to use data from a table, such as question 1 (Figure 15.2), it is important that you only use the part of the table relevant to the question – otherwise you may waste valuable time providing information that has not been requested.

Back to ...

The NWW Coursemates website to check your answers to the exam practice question.

16
The growth of settlements

⇨ *The New Wider World*, pp34–41

KEY IDEAS

1 Physical and economic factors can influence the location and growth of settlements.

2 Settlements have a range of functions.

3 Settlements can be arranged in a hierarchy.

Key words to know

Settlement
Site
Physical factors
Location
Economic factors
Defensive site
Bridging point

Back to ...

The New Wider World
pp40–41 for details on how to extract information on settlements from an OS map.

The New Wider World
pp34–35 for more information on site factors.

Key words to know

Sphere of influence
Threshold
Range

---

1 Physical and economic factors can influence the location and growth of settlements

A **settlement** is a place where people live. The term can be applied to a small collection of houses (a hamlet) or a city with a population of millions. The size of any settlement will be influenced by the site and location of the settlement.

The **site** of the settlement refers to the characteristics of where it is located. **Physical factors** such as shelter, defence and water supply (wet point site) were historically important in choosing the initial site. However, a good **location** was important if the settlement was to have the potential for further growth. The location of a settlement describes where it is in relation to surrounding features such as other settlements, mountains, rivers and communications. For example, Belfast is located:

- on an area of flat land
- between Divis Mountain to the west and the Castlereagh Hills to the east
- at the mouth of the River Lagan
- at the junction of the M1 and M2 motorways
- 18 km south-west of Carrickfergus and 14 km north-east of Lisburn.

A favourable location would possess economic benefits, e.g. a reliable food supply, mineral or timber resources and good communications. Many settlements in Northern Ireland still display evidence of the physical or economic factors which encouraged their early growth. For example:

- Carrickfergus developed in the twelfth century as the Normans believed it was a good **defensive site** (Figure 16.1).
- Enniskillen (Figure 16.2), Banbridge and Coleraine are located at the **bridging point** of rivers. This is where a river could be crossed most easily.
- Belfast and Derry developed as ports as they were sited at the furthest point inland to which ships could travel safely.

In some instances the physical or economic factors that influenced the location of settlements are still visible and can be identified on Ordnance Survey (OS) maps, for example the presence of a stream or river to supply water.

It is also possible to measure the growth in settlements over time by making comparisons with older maps. However, it is important to remember that maps may have different scales.

Figure 16.1
Carrickfergus on the shores of Belfast Lough – a defensive site

Figure 16.2
Enniskillen – a bridging point

Check this!...

1   Identify three physical factors that would be important in choosing a site for a settlement.

2   Using the example of Belfast as a guide, describe the location of the settlement you live in.

2 Settlements have a range of functions

As settlements grow they develop a number of **functions**. These are the main activities of the settlement (Figure 16.3). In some cases, the original function may no longer be applicable, e.g. Carrickfergus no longer has a defensive function (Figure 16.1). In other cases, functions have changed over a period of time, e.g. Whitehead on the shores of Belfast Lough was at one time a popular tourist resort but it is now a dormitory town for Belfast.

Key word to know

Function

Figure 16.3 Types of function

Function	Description	Northern Ireland example
Market towns	Originally collecting and distribution centres for surrounding farming area. Today they may service and process agricultural machinery and produce.	Cookstown
Mining towns	Developed to exploit local mineral or fuels.	Coalisland
Industrial/manufacturing	Where raw materials are processed into manufactured goods.	Lisburn
Ports	Located on coasts, rivers and lakes for the movement of goods and people from land to sea, or vice versa.	Larne
Route centres	At the convergence of several natural routes or at nodal points resulting from economic development.	Ballymena
Commercial	Providing the needs of industry and business.	Belfast
Educational/cultural/religious	Attracting people, perhaps for a short period, for educational and religious purposes.	Derry
Residential	Where the majority of residents live but do not work.	Whitehead
Tourist resorts	Include spa towns, coastal and mountain resorts.	Newcastle (County Down)

3 Settlements can be arranged in a hierarchy

The term **hierarchy** refers to the arrangement of settlements within a given area (e.g. a country or county) in an 'order of importance'. Isolated farms and small hamlets form the base of the hierarchy pyramid, with the largest and/or capital city at the top. Three criteria have been suggested to determine the order of importance in the hierarchy of settlements: population, range and number of services, and market area.

Key word to know

Hierarchy

The population size of a settlement

Early attempts to determine a settlement hierarchy were based on size. However, no one has been able to produce a widely accepted division between, for example, a hamlet and a village, or a village and a town. Indeed, so-called villages in places like India and China are often as large as many British towns. However, large settlements tend to be fewer in number and further apart than smaller ones, e.g. the two largest settlements in Northern Ireland, Belfast and Derry, are 115 km apart.

The range and number of services provided by a settlement

Villages provide a limited range and number of services. Services that do exist are those likely to be used daily (the village shop) or which reduce the need to travel to other places (a primary school). In Figure 16.4, where the hierarchy is based on services, each place in the hierarchy is likely to have all the services of settlements below them.

Figure 16.4 Hierarchy of settlements based on services

Capital e.g. Belfast	Cathedrals, government buildings, banking HQ, railway termini, museums and art galleries, large theatre, shopping centre, several universities, international airport
City e.g. Derry	Large railway station, large shopping complex, cathedral, opticians and jewellers, large hospital, university, theatre, airport
Large town e.g. Ballymena	Several shopping areas/arcades, railway station, bus station, hotels, banks, small hospital
Small town e.g. Castlederg	Town hall, doctor, several churches/chapels, cafés and restaurants, small secondary school, bus station, several shops
Village e.g. Ballycarry	Church, post office, public house, shop for daily goods, small primary school, village hall
Hamlet	Perhaps none, or public telephone

Figure 16.5 Threshold population for selected services

Service	Threshold population
Small grocery shop	350
Doctor's surgery	2500
Secondary school	10 000
Marks and Spencer	50 000
Sainsbury's	60 000

Back to …

The New Wider World
p38 Figure 3.14 for a map of Exeter's sphere of influence.

The sphere of influence, or market area, of a settlement

The **sphere of influence** may be defined as the area served by a particular settlement. The area of the sphere of influence depends upon the size and services of a town and its surrounding settlements, the transport facilities available and the level of competition from rival settlements.

The size of the sphere of influence is closely related to threshold and range:

- The **threshold** population is the minimum number of people needed to ensure that demand is large enough for a special service to be offered to the people living in that area. Figure 16.5 explains why there are countless small grocery shops but only eight Sainsbury's supermarkets located in Northern Ireland.
- **Range** is the maximum distance that people are prepared to travel to obtain a service. People will only travel short distances for everyday basic needs but are willing to travel much further for a special purpose, e.g. to attend a concert at the Odyssey Arena in Belfast.

Check this!…

1 What is the function of a settlement?

2 Identify three ways of arranging settlements in a hierarchy.

3 Explain why a shoe shop will have a larger range, sphere of influence and threshold population than a corner/village shop.

1 State the meaning of the term *location*.   (2 marks)

2 Using Figure 16.1 on page 102, state fully one reason why Carrickfergus was a good defensive site.   (3 marks)

Use Figure 16.6 to answer questions 3 and 4.

3 Which settlement will have a larger sphere of influence?   (1 mark)

4 Explain your answer to question 3.   (3 marks)

Figure 16.6 Information for two settlements in County Fermanagh

	Enniskillen	Lisnaskea
Population	11 425	2430
Secondary schools	8	2
Supermarkets	7	2
Churches	8	4
Cinemas	1	0
Hospitals	1	0

EXAM TIPS

Photographs such as Figure 16.1 may be used as a resource for an exam question. Study the photograph carefully, including looking for background features that may be important, when using it to answer the question.

Back to ...

The NWW Coursemates website to check your answers to the exam practice question.

⇨ *The New Wider World*, pp78–88

KEY IDEAS

1 Urbanisation occurs due to migration and natural increase in population.

2 Models can be used to describe urban land use.

3 MEDC and LEDC cities have contrasting urban structures.

4 Changes in urban areas can have positive and negative impacts.

Key words to know

Urbanisation
Rural
Urban

Back to ...

Figure 10.1 on page 61 shows the location of some of the world's largest cities.

1 Urbanisation occurs due to migration and natural increase in population

Urbanisation is a process whereby the proportion of people living in towns and cities increases. Urbanisation can result from two processes:

- Migration from the countryside or **rural** areas to the built-up **urban** areas of towns and cities is greater than the flow of migrants from urban to rural areas.
- Natural population increase is greater in the urban areas.

In 1800 only 3 per cent of the world's population lived in urban areas. By 1950 this proportion had risen to 29 per cent and is predicted to exceed 50 per cent by the year 2006.

Million cities and megacities

The process of urbanisation has led to the growth of very large cities with a population exceeding 1 million. In 1850 there were only two 'million cities' – London and Paris. This number increased to 70 by 1950 and is expected to reach 543 by 2015.

A new term, megacity, refers to places with a population in excess of 10 million. There were five megacities in 1975 but the United Nations Habitat group predict that this number will reach 21 by 2015.

Rank order	1970	1985	2000
1	New York 16.5	Tokyo 23.0	Tokyo 27.0
2	Tokyo 13.4	Mexico City 18.7	São Paulo 16.6
3	London 10.5	New York 18.2	New York 16.4
4	Shanghai 10.0	São Paulo 16.8	Mexico City 15.9
5	Mexico City 8.6	Shanghai 13.3	Mumbai (Bombay) 15.4
6	Los Angeles 8.4	Los Angeles 12.8	Shanghai 15.3
7	Buenos Aires 8.4	Buenos Aires 11.6	Beijing 12.7
8	Paris 8.4	Rio De Janeiro 11.1	Los Angeles 12.5
9	São Paulo 7.1	Kolkata (Calcutta) 9.2	Kolkata 11.8
10	Moscow 7.1	Mumbai 8.2	Seoul 11.7 } Jakarta 11.7 }

Figure 17.1 The world's largest cities (populations in millions)

Figure 17.1 shows the changing location of the world's largest cities. In 1970 five of the largest cities were in the MEDCs but by 2000 there were only three. These figures reflect the dramatic increase in million cities in developing countries, the majority of which lie within the tropics.

Contrasting rates of urbanisation

Figure 17.2 shows that in 1950 over 50 per cent of the population in the MEDCs already lived in urban areas and, while this figure has increased in the intervening period, the rate of increase has slowed. Most MEDCs experienced urbanisation in the early 1800s at a time of rapid industrial growth. The rural unemployment created by the mechanisation of farming in the 1800s acted as a push factor while the attraction of jobs in the factories, mines and shipyards created an urban pull factor. As death rates were high in the urban areas during this time, natural increase was not a significant factor in the process of urbanisation.

Rural to urban migration still continues, especially from remote rural areas where there is a lack of opportunities and services, but at a much lower rate. The slow-down towards the end of the twentieth century has been attributed to an out-migration from large cities to smaller towns and rural districts, a process known as **counterurbanisation**.

In contrast to MEDCs, the rate of urbanisation in the LEDCs is increasing rapidly. Most of the economic opportunities available are concentrated in the cities, attracting young people like a magnet. This rural to urban migration has been a driving force of the rapid rate of urbanisation in the LEDCs (Figure 17.3).

Unfortunately, as shown in Figure 17.4, many of the urban pull factors exist only in the minds of the migrants and the reality they find on arrival is very different.

Death rates have fallen faster in urban areas because of better access to health services, but birth rates are still relatively high in most LEDCs and therefore the rates of natural increase are also quite high in cities.

Key words to know

Counterurbanisation

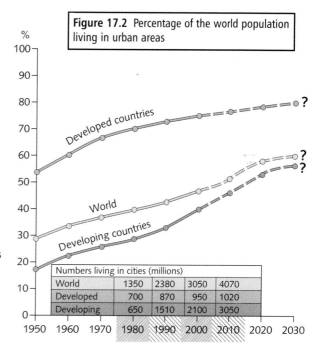

Figure 17.2 Percentage of the world population living in urban areas

Numbers living in cities (millions)				
World	1350	2380	3050	4070
Developed	700	870	950	1020
Developing	650	1510	2100	3050

Figure 17.3 Urbanisation can result in sprawling cities

Back to ...

The New Wider World **p78**
Figure 5.2 for a map
showing world urban
population.

Figure 17.4 Rural 'push' and urban 'pull' factors

Check this!...

1 What causes urbanisation?

2 Where are most of the million cities now located?

3 Explain why rates of urbanisation are much higher in the LEDCs than in the MEDCs.

Key words to know

Land use zone
Functional zone
Central business district (CBD)
Residential zone
Bid-rent
Socio-economic

2 Models can be used to describe urban land use

Although each urban area is unique, with its own distinctive pattern, it is likely to share common **land use** or **functional zones** which may include shops, parks and a variety of housing types. Two of the earliest models of land use zones to be put forward, and which are still the easiest to apply, are shown in Figure 17.5. A model is a theoretical framework which may not actually exist, but which helps to explain the reality.

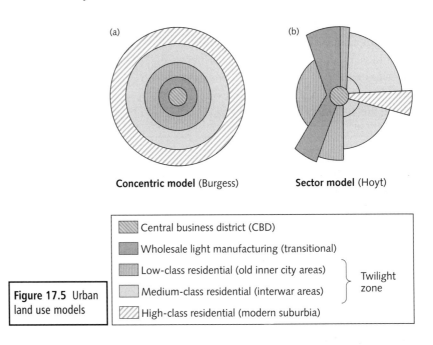

Concentric model (Burgess)   Sector model (Hoyt)

▨	Central business district (CBD)
▦	Wholesale light manufacturing (transitional)
▥	Low-class residential (old inner city areas)
▤	Medium-class residential (interwar areas)
▨	High-class residential (modern suburbia)

Twilight zone

Figure 17.5 Urban land use models

← **Back to ...**

The New Wider World **p81**
Figure 5.9 for a model of land use in an LEDC city.

- Burgess claimed that in the centre of all towns and cities there was a **central business district (CBD)**. He suggested, initially using Chicago as his example, that towns grew outwards from this CBD in a concentric pattern. The three **residential zones** were based on the age of houses and the wealth of their occupants.
- Hoyt proposed his model after the development of public transport. He suggested that urban areas developed in sectors, or wedges, alongside main transport routes into and out of a city.

It is important to note that both the Burgess and Hoyt models are based on settlements within MEDCs and therefore do not include reference to the different processes at work within LEDC cities.

Urban land use and functional zones

Each of the land use zones shown in Figure 17.5 has a function. The four main types of function are shops and offices, industry, housing, and open space. The location and the distribution of each land use or functional zone are related to several factors:

- **Land values and space** Land values are highest and available sites more limited in the CBD where competition for land is greatest. This is explained by the **bid-rent** theory which states that the highest bidder will acquire the use of the land and the reason they pay the most is because they can obtain maximum profit from that land.
- **Age** As towns developed outwards, the oldest buildings were near to the city centre (although many of these have now been replaced) and the newest ones in the outskirts.
- **Accessibility** The CBD, where the main routes from the suburbs and surrounding towns meet, has traditionally been the easiest place to reach from all parts of the city although this ease is now often reduced due to increased congestion.
- **Socio-economic characteristics of the inhabitants** People with the same social or economic status tend to group together. Poorer members of the community tend to live in cheaper housing near to the CBD (with its shops) and in the inner city (where most jobs used to be found).
- **Changes in demand** Land use and function change with time. For example, the main land use demand in the nineteenth century was for industry and low-cost housing. Today it is for industry, shops and better-quality housing, all in a more pleasant environment, and open space.

Check this!...

1 Why is the Burgess model laid out in concentric circles?

2 Describe fully one difference between the Burgess and Hoyt models.

3 Explain how land values can determine the location of functional zones.

3 MEDC and LEDC cities have contrasting urban structures

MEDCs and LEDCs have both experienced urbanisation but the urban structures created are in many ways very different. This can be attributed to the fact that urbanisation occurred at different times in history, at different rates, and had different causes in the MEDCs and the LEDCs. The urban structures of Rio de Janeiro (Brazil) and Belfast (Northern Ireland) are used here to exemplify these contrasts.

Case Study Extra

Rio de Janeiro – the urban structure of an LEDC city

Rio de Janeiro is situated around the huge natural harbour of Guanabara Bay in south-east Brazil. Although it was replaced by Brasilia as the country's capital in 1960 and by São Paulo as the centre of industry and commerce, Rio is still one of the world's largest cities. In 2002, some 6 million people lived in the main urban area and 10 million in the metropolitan region (Figure 17.6).

- Rio does not conform to the models of urban development in Figure 17.5, as the central business district is surrounded by a zone of luxury apartments. This area is popular with the wealthy residents of Rio as it is close to all the functions of the CBD and beaches like Copacabana, and has a much better infrastructure than those areas further away from the centre. This area still contains some favelas which are informal settlements or **shanty towns** which may lack basic services, but they should not be confused with slum dwellings which are neglected. One such favela exists at Copacabana's Leme Beach where it extends up the hillside just three blocks from luxury hotels.

- Approximately one-third of the population live in the older inner suburbs which are built on the flat tidal plains. This zone comprises typical middle-income and low-income family homes as well as the majority of the favelas, including the largest favela ➤

> in Brazil – Roçinha, home to over 100 000 people. Traditional and modern industries are also located in this zone.
- The newer outer suburbs are largely composed of low-class housing and the open spaces represent the greatest growth area for new favelas. The level of poverty in this zone can be identified through the proportion of households receiving less than $120/month (the Brazilian definition of poverty). In the industrial city of Nova Iguaçu on the edge of the Rio metropolitan area this figure is 33 per cent. The provision of basic services such as water, electricity and sanitation is very poor here. This zone marks the edge of the commuter zone. **Commuters** are people who make a journey from home to work each day. The poor transport infrastructure and high costs make commuting very difficult for anyone living beyond the outer suburbs.
- The urban–rural fringe is the least urbanised of the zones and is composed mostly of lower-class housing.

The urban structure of Rio shows a strong element of division based on levels of income. This division of groups is called **segregation** and although in this case it is based on income, it can also be based on race, religion or age. The most affluent inhabitants live in the central areas while the poorest live mainly in areas furthest from the city centre.

Using your case study
You need to know the pattern of land use in Rio de Janeiro (an LEDC city) and contrast it with an MEDC city (Belfast).

Case study links
This case study of an LEDC city should be used in conjunction with the MEDC case study of Belfast.

Key words to know

Shanty town
Commuter
Segregation

Back to...

The New Wider World **pp86–88** for a detailed case study of Rio de Janeiro.

Learn it!

1 Explain why Rio de Janeiro does not conform to the urban models in Figure 17.5

2 Suggest why most new favelas are located on the outskirts of the city.

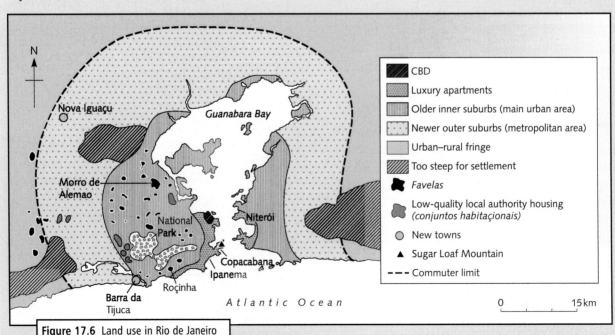

Figure 17.6 Land use in Rio de Janeiro

N

Nova Iguaçu

Guanabara Bay

Morro de Alemao

National Park

Niterói

Copacabana
Ipanema

Roçinha

Barra da Tijuca

Atlantic Ocean

0   15km

CBD
Luxury apartments
Older inner suburbs (main urban area)
Newer outer suburbs (metropolitan area)
Urban–rural fringe
Too steep for settlement
Favelas
Low-quality local authority housing (*conjuntos habitaçionais*)
New towns
▲ Sugar Loaf Mountain
- - - Commuter limit

Belfast – the urban structure of an MEDC city

Key words to know

Key words to know

Green belt
Urban sprawl
Ethnic

Despite a falling population in recent decades (Figure 17.7), Belfast remains the second largest city in the whole of Ireland behind Dublin which has a population of 1 million.

Year	Population
1951	443 671
1971	416 679
1981	295 223
1991	279 237
2001	277 391

Figure 17.7 Population change in Belfast

The growth of Belfast (Figure 17.8) has been shaped by the physical geography of the site. Over the last century the city has spread to the north-east along the shores of Belfast Lough, through the Dundonald Gap to the east and along the course of the River Lagan to the south-east.

The structure of the city shows some similarities to both the Burgess and Hoyt models.

- Due to the high cost of land, the central business district has the tallest buildings which house offices, car parks, shops and services. In theory, this is the most accessible part of the city as rail and bus routes and the main roads converge here. However, accessibility has been adversely affected by increasing levels of traffic congestion over recent years.
- The industrial areas in Belfast do not surround the CBD but are concentrated in sectors along the shores of Belfast Lough –

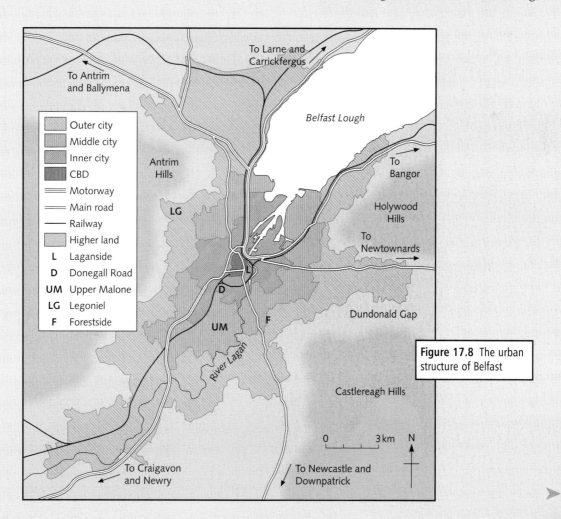

Figure 17.8 The urban structure of Belfast

Legend:
- Outer city
- Middle city
- Inner city
- CBD
- Motorway
- Main road
- Railway
- Higher land
- **L** Laganside
- **D** Donegall Road
- **UM** Upper Malone
- **LG** Legoniel
- **F** Forestside

comparable to the Hoyt model. Industry can also be found in new, purpose-built units on the edge of the city.

- Much of the terraced housing of the old inner city area, which surrounds the CBD, has been redeveloped. Some streets of terraced housing remain, e.g. Donegall Road, but much of the 'two up–two down' housing has been replaced by lower-density housing with space allocated for gardens and car parking. New luxury apartments have been built in this zone as part of the Laganside scheme.
- The growth of what is described in Figure 17.5 as medium-class housing grew in sectors along the main transport routes into the city. These housing areas were served by trams from 1872 and buses from 1926.
- The edge of the city is dominated by residential development which has occurred since the 1950s, e.g. Upper Malone and Legoniel. The urban models of Figure 17.5 classify these suburbs as high-class residential areas, but in Belfast this is not

always the case. While the housing is of a lower density than the zones closer to the CBD, the type of housing can vary greatly. The suburbs contain council housing estates which were built for lower-income groups to rent, as well as luxury developments aimed at the private buyer. Shopping centres to rival the CBD have been built in this zone, e.g. Forestside. The growth of the suburbs is constrained by what planners call a **green belt**. The aim of this planning restriction is to conserve land for agricultural and leisure purposes as well as the character of surrounding towns and villages which can become part of the city through **urban sprawl**.

Apart from the socio-economic segregation described above, many residential areas of Belfast are also segregated along religious or **ethnic** lines (Figure 17.9). Various names can be used to describe the two groupings:

- Roman Catholic/Irish Nationalist/Irish Republican
- Protestant/Ulster Unionist/Loyalist.

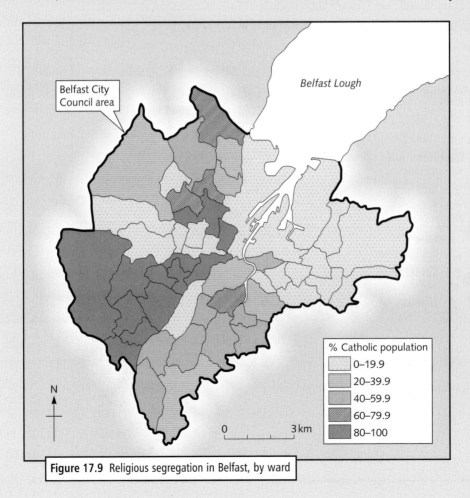

Figure 17.9 Religious segregation in Belfast, by ward

Segregation can occur for positive reasons, e.g. proximity to place of worship (church or chapel) or negative reasons, e.g. fear, intimidation and violence.

In parts of the city where violence has flared between the two groups, different types of physical barrier have been constructed, rather inappropriately named 'Peace Walls' (Figure 17.10).

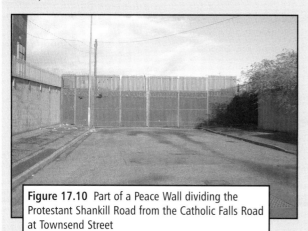

Figure 17.10 Part of a Peace Wall dividing the Protestant Shankill Road from the Catholic Falls Road at Townsend Street

Using your case study
You need to know the pattern of land use in Belfast (an MEDC city) and contrast it with an LEDC city (Rio de Janeiro).

Case study links
This case study of an MEDC city should be used in conjunction with the case study of Rio de Janeiro, an LEDC city.

Learn it!

1 Why did Belfast's middle-class residential areas grow in sectors?

2 Why have Peace Walls (Figure 17.10) been built?

3 Suggest which groups may oppose or support the green belt.

4 Changes in urban areas can have positive and negative impacts

Urban growth in the LEDCs has been so fast that the cities have not been able to cope with the rapid increase in population. Over 100 million people living in developing cities have no shelter of any kind, while over one-third live in squatter settlements – sites that were only vacant because they are subject to flooding, landslips or industrial pollution. Although most local authorities would probably prefer to remove shanty settlements from their cities, few have the necessary resources that would be needed to provide alternative accommodation. As a result, shanty settlements become permanent. Self-help schemes seem, therefore, the only hope for the squatters to improve their homes.

Case Study

Urban change in Rio de Janeiro

Back to...

The New Wider World **pp86–88** for the case study of Rio de Janeiro.

The desire for improved living conditions has led to a number of changes in Rio. Many of the wealthier residents have moved out of the city to the new town of Barra da Tijuca in an attempt to find more space and a safer place to live, while the residents of the favelas are attempting to upgrade their homes through self-help schemes.

Using your case study
You can use this case study to answer questions on urban change in an LEDC city. You should be able to identify:
- the causes of the changes, e.g. a desire for better-quality housing
- the impacts of the changes on the people and the environment (positive

➤ and negative), e.g. improved living standards

● how the change was managed, e.g. the work of residents' associations.

Case study links

The changes described in this case study relate to the urban structure of Rio described on page 110.

Update

Go to *The NWW Coursemates* website for a link to Global Eye and follow links to the Summer 2002 edition for further details of urban change in Rio.

Learn it!

1 Describe three improvements carried out in Roçinha.

2 How is the work of the favela improvement scheme restricted?

3 Explain how the changes have had a positive impact on the local people and environment.

Urban change in the UK

Changes in the CBD

Before the rapid growth of urban areas in nineteenth-century Britain, most town centres were dominated by open-air markets selling animals, farm produce and household goods. By the twentieth century the most important types of land use in the CBD had become shops, offices and commercial buildings. City centres also came to include places of entertainment (theatres and cinemas), culture (museums and art galleries) and public buildings (town or city hall). The CBD, because it was most accessible for everyone living in and around the town or city, became the most frequently visited and, consequently, the busiest area. As a result:

● the narrow streets, built before the invention of the car, bus and delivery lorry, were often congested
● the large volume of traffic caused air pollution and was a danger to the health and safety of shoppers and other pedestrians
● there was insufficient space for car parks, and buses found it difficult to keep to time
● larger shops moved out and re-located on less congested sites in either old inner city areas (e.g. DIY, furniture and carpet shops) or on the rural–urban fringe (e.g. electrical shops and hypermarkets)
● there was a need for modern, carefully planned city centres that considered social, economic and environmental needs.

Many city centres have had to undergo several changes in an attempt to reduce the loss of shops, hotels and offices to out-of-town locations. These include the creation of pedestrianised areas and, later, the development of shopping malls. These changes were aimed at improving the quality of the urban environment and making shopping in this area a more convenient and enjoyable experience.

More recently has come an increased demand for:

● a more relaxing atmosphere within the city centre
● an increase in leisure amenities, especially in the evenings.

This is being achieved by:

● providing sitting areas, erecting hanging baskets, planting flower beds and shrubs and adding small areas of grass

- providing cafés with outside tables, small restaurants and theme bars
- employing more staff to ensure that the place is kept clean and undamaged.

Changes in old inner city areas

Most inner city areas developed along with industry in the nineteenth century. As industry grew, so too did the demand for workers. As an increasing number of people moved from rural areas to the towns for work, they needed low-cost houses in which to live. At that time, without either public or private transport, people also wanted to live as close as possible to their place of work.

Over the years, attempts have been made to improve living conditions, initially – as in the 1960s – by bulldozing large areas (slum clearance) and building high-rise flats (urban redevelopment) and later by improving existing properties (urban renewal).

Inner cities were characterised by large factories built during the Industrial Revolution. They were located:

- on the nearest available land to the town centre and where there was enough space for large buildings
- next to canals and, after the 1840s, railways which were needed to transport the heavy and bulky raw materials and the finished manufactured goods
- beside rivers which, initially used as a source of power, provided water for washing and cooling and a means of disposing of waste
- next to land that could be used to house the large number of workers who were needed.

Since then many factories have been forced to close either due to a lack of space for expansion and modernisation, or due to narrow, congested roads. Some factories, like the terraced housing, have been left empty, while others have been pulled down to leave large areas of derelict land.

Changes at the rural–urban fringe

In an attempt to control the rapid urban growth of the 1920s and 1930s, green belts were created by Act of Parliament in 1947. Planning permission was normally not meant to be granted for development proposals within the green belt but in reality planners often came under considerable pressure to release land for more housing, jobs and roads.

At the start of the twenty-first century the government faces mounting pressure to release more green belt land for development. The main reasons are that at the fringe there is:

- cheaper land
- less traffic congestion and pollution
- a better road infrastructure that gives easier access to surrounding settlements and other urban areas
- a pleasanter environment with more open space.

Check this!...

1 Why have pedestrian areas been created in many city centres?

2 Identify two reasons why industry has moved away from the old inner city areas.

Urban change in Belfast

Belfast has a rich industrial heritage but recent decades have seen a decline in the manufacturing sector (Figure 17.11) which has affected the geography of the city.

Year	Secondary (%)	Tertiary (%)
1961	48.3	51.7
1971	39.9	60.1
1981	29.5	70.5
1991	19.1	80.9
2001	11.8	88.2

Figure 17.11 Belfast's changing employment structure

Causes of change

The decline in Belfast's industrial base can be attributed to four factors:

1 Loss of markets, e.g. Gallaher's cigarette factory (see Chapter 13 page 86) suffered through a change in smoking habits.

2 Overseas competition, e.g. Korean shipyards are more competitive as labour is cheaper.

3 Economic recession has resulted in job losses, e.g. aircraft manufacturing at Shorts/Bombardier.

4 New innovations reduced the demand for linen, e.g. the development of synthetic fibres such as nylon.

	Positive	Negative
Effects on people	● Redundancy payments may be used to start new businesses.	● Young people may find it difficult to secure employment on leaving school. ● Older people may find it difficult to get a new job.
Effects on the environment	● Redeveloping existing industrial or brownfield sites reduces pressure on the green belt. ● Reduction in air and noise pollution.	● Derelict factories create a source of visual pollution. ● Old industrial sites, e.g. the gasworks, can be expensive to clean up.

Figure 17.12 The effects of deindustrialisation in Belfast

Impacts of change

Management response

● Making Belfast Work was launched in 1988 to strengthen the efforts being made to address the economic, educational, social, health and environmental problems facing the people of Belfast. Up to 2003, £310 million had been spent supporting over 500 projects.

● The Industrial Development Board (IDB) was formed by the government in 1982 to promote economic growth across Northern Ireland. It was replaced in 2002 by Invest N.I. as the main economic development organisation. This organisation seeks to obtain inward investment as well as encouraging the development of home-grown industries.

● The Laganside Corporation was set up by the government in 1989 to secure the regeneration of Belfast's riverside and waterfront areas.

Back to...

Chapter 18 pages 119–121 for further details on the Laganside scheme.

Using your case study

You can us this case study to answer questions on urban change in an MEDC city. You should be able to identify:

● the causes of the changes
● the impacts of the changes on the people and the environment (positive and negative)
● how each change was managed.

Case study links

This case study links with the case study of change in function of industrial premises on page 86.

Update

Go to *The NWW Coursemates* website for a link to the Belfast Telegraph and use the archive service to look for recent articles on industrial change.

Learn it!

1 What are the causes of the industrial decline in Belfast?

2 Describe two impacts of this change.

3 How has the government managed this change?

1 State the meaning of the term *urbanisation*.
(2 marks)

2 State fully two pull factors that may cause a rise in the urban population. (4 marks)

3 Explain why Hoyt believed that urban growth would occur in sectors. (2 marks)

4 Figure 17.10 shows part of a Peace Line segregating two residential areas in Belfast. Give two reasons why segregation may occur.
(4 marks)

5 For an MEDC city that you have studied, state fully two ways in which land use differs from the Burgess model shown in Figure 17.5. (6 marks)

EXAM TIPS

Many candidates mistakenly think that *urbanisation* means a growth in the urban population, rather than an increase in the proportion of people living in urban areas. As a result they lose marks in exams. Make sure that you know the difference.

Back to ...

The NWW Coursemates website to check your answers to the exam practice question.

KEY IDEAS

1 Planning initiatives in the inner cities can help to create sustainable urban environments.

2 Inner city redevelopment creates problems and benefits for local communities.

3 Sustainable cities require management of traffic and waste problems.

Key words to know

Planning
Sustainable urban environment
Regenerate

1 Planning initiatives in the inner cities can help to create sustainable urban environments

Planning is an important aspect of urban change as it ensures that change occurs in an organised and structured way to best meet the needs of the population. If cities are to continue to meet the needs of future generations, planners must seek to develop **sustainable urban environments**. The URBAN21 Conference held in 2000 defined sustainable urban development as:

'Improving the quality of life in a city ... without leaving a burden on the future generations.'

Planning initiatives can play a key role in achieving the characteristics of a more sustainable urban environment, as listed in Figure 18.1.

More sustainable	Less sustainable
Compact forms of residential development.	Low-density, spread-out residential development.
Mixed land use; homes, jobs and shopping in close proximity.	Segregation of land uses: homes, jobs and shopping separated into uniform tracts or concentrations.
Employment based primarily on education and skills.	Employment based primarily on environment-polluting or non-renewable resource based industries.
Movement on foot and by bicycle.	Heavy dependence on private cars.
Wind and solar energy.	Fossil fuel based energy.
Tertiary treatment of sewage; use of natural means of sewage treatment.	Discharge of sewage into water bodies or water-courses untreated or with low level of treatment.
Protection and use of natural hydrologic systems.	Hard surfaces preventing infiltration; channelling of natural water-courses.
Natural open space; protection of wetlands, woodlands, stream valleys, habitats, etc.; use of manure, compost, integrated pest management, etc.	Destruction of natural landscape; 'manicured' parkland with exotic species; heavy use of chemical fertilisers, herbicides, pesticides.
Reduction of waste; recovery, re-use and recycling of waste materials.	Landfills, incinerators.

Figure 18.1 Checklist for sustainable settlements

Inner city redevelopment

Like many industrial cities across the UK, Belfast's inner city was characterised by high-density housing, industries and transport corridors carrying roads and railways and the River Lagan. This was an important area for the industrial growth of the city but by the 1980s the inner city was an area of dereliction, pollution and outmigration. At this time the government set up Urban Development Corporations (UDCs) in an attempt to **regenerate** those inner city areas that had large amounts of derelict and unused land and buildings. UDCs had the power to acquire, reclaim and use land and to convert buildings. By encouraging private-sector investment, UDCs were able to promote industrial, housing and community developments.

The first two UDCs, the London Docklands Development Corporation (LDDC) and the Merseyside Development Corporation (MDC), came into existence in 1981. In Northern Ireland the process of planning for the redevelopment of the inner city areas along the River Lagan began in 1987. This process allowed all groups that might be affected by the changes to have their say in the way that the plan was formulated. The Laganside Corporation was set up by the government in 1989 to implement this plan.

Back to ...

The New Wider World **p60** for information on the London Docklands Development Corporation.

Check this!...

1 What is sustainable urban development?
2 Identify the aims of UDCs.

Case Study Extra

Urban regeneration at Laganside

Improving the River Lagan

The Laganside Corporation was originally given the task of redeveloping an area along a 4.8 km stretch of the River Lagan. The area for redevelopment was expanded in 1997 to include a 200 hectare site known as the Cathedral Quarter.

The success of the scheme depended on improving the quality of the environment and in particular the River Lagan. The water quality in the river was very poor due to:

● the large amount of domestic pollution entering the river
● denser seawater getting trapped under the river water – this stagnant seawater reduced the oxygen levels of the water and encouraged decomposition of the mudflats which gave off a bad smell when exposed at low tide (Figure 18.2).

These problems were tackled by:

● upgrading the sewage system
● installing a riverbed aeration scheme to pump 350 kg of oxygen into the river every day.
● building the Lagan Weir at the cost of £14 million to ensure that the mudflats are covered at all times thereby creating a more attractive residential and recreational environment (the weir was officially opened in March 1994)
● periodical dredging of the river.

New pathways were built along the river to allow people access to the revitalised river. The pathways include areas of greenery which support the development of wildlife habitats. There are also a number of pieces of public art along the pathways.

Figure 18.2 The exposed mudflats of the River Lagan

Figure 18.3 The Lagan Weir

Improving buildings

The Belfast gasworks closed in 1988 after serving the city for over 150 years, leaving a heavily polluted site. The soil could not be cleaned so it was removed and the site has been attractively landscaped. The character of this part of Belfast will be maintained by the conservation of the gasworks office with its distinctive clock tower, the ornate Meter House and the Klondyke building.

Improving transport links

Two new bridges were built across the Lagan as part of the redevelopment scheme to solve long-standing transport problems. The Dargan rail bridge (Figure 18.4) which connects the Larne railway line to the lines to Bangor and Dublin, and the Lagan road bridge which links the M2 with the Sydenham bypass, were both opened in 1995 by Queen Elizabeth.

Figure 18.4 The Dargan rail bridge – the Lagan road bridge is immediately behind it

Creating world-class amenities

Amenities are the features of an environment which make it pleasant or attractive. The Laganside scheme has brought a number of new amenities to this part of Belfast, including the following:

- The Waterfront Hall is a 2000-seater concert and conference venue which was built at the cost of £32 million.
- The Odyssey Arena (Figure 18.5) contains a diverse range of attractions, e.g. an IMAX theatre, multiplex cinema, shops, bars, restaurants and a ten-pin bowling alley. The centrepiece is the 10 000-seater arena which has hosted concerts by some of the top names in the music business as well as being home to the Belfast Giants ice hockey team.
- The Cathedral Quarter includes a Writer's Square which can accommodate up to 1000 people for outdoor events.
- St George's Market, one of Belfast's best-known landmarks, has been revitalised by a £4.5 million refurbishment and renovation scheme. Such has been the new-found popularity of the market that there is now a waiting list of some 60 traders seeking access to it.

Figure 18.5 The Odyssey Arena

New housing for the inner city

> **Key word to know**
>
> *Gentrification*

One of the most striking features of the Laganside development is the large number of apartments which have been built along the Lagan (Figure 18.6). Their attractive views over the river and their proximity to the city centre make them desirable properties – especially for those working in the city.

Figure 18.6 Apartments beside the River Lagan

Properties in this area come at a high price, with most apartments costing over £100 000 and as a result the area is changing in character. This process of housing improvement is having an effect on the neighbour composition, with lower-income groups being replaced by more affluent people, usually in professional or managerial occupations. This process is known as **gentrification**.

Employment opportunities

Employment in this area is now dominated by service (tertiary) industries. A total of £710 million of investment has brought about 10 000 jobs into the Laganside area. Some of the employers are listed in Figure 18.7.

Location	Employer
Lanyon Place	Fujitsu (400 jobs) Hilton Hotel (225 jobs) BT (1200 jobs)
Gasworks	Halifax (1500 jobs) (Figure 18.8) Radisson SAS Hotel (80 jobs)
Abercorn Basin	Odyssey Arena (600 jobs)
Clarendon Dock	Prudential (500 jobs) Zurich Insurance (138 jobs)

Figure 18.7 Some of the major employers on Laganside

Figure 18.8 The Halifax call centre at the Gasworks site

Using your case study

Laganside is an example of a planning initiative at the local/small scale. You should have knowledge of the measures taken to regenerate and improve this area of Belfast, e.g. new amenities including the Odyssey Arena and Waterfront Hall. It is important that you are able to evaluate the measures taken to regenerate this area in terms of the benefits and problems for local communities.

Update

Go to *The NWW Coursemates* website for a link to Laganside for the latest information on developments or special events in this area.

Learn it!

1 Explain why the area of Laganside was unattractive before development.

2 How did the Lagan Weir improve the environmental quality of Laganside?

3 Describe two new amenities that have been built on Laganside.

2 Inner city redevelopment creates problems and benefits for local communities

The redevelopment of Laganside has transformed the area in terms of housing, jobs, amenities and quality of the environment, but the local **community** has expressed concern over the changes. The local community is composed of people who have lived in this area for a long period of time and have a shared interest in the future well-being of the area. Their concerns focus on:

- the price of houses and apartments which are too expensive for local people to purchase and consequently they have to move elsewhere
- the new residents, who are young and upwardly mobile, thereby changing the social character of the area
- a lack of appreciation of the history of the area among the new residents, with the result that the sense of community is dying out
- the lack of employment opportunities for local people in the new businesses that have come to Laganside.

Key words to know

Community

The Laganside Corporation is seeking to address these concerns to ensure that local communities benefit from the changes brought about by the redevelopment. Laganside has worked closely with employers, the Training and Employment Agency and community groups to provide training schemes linked to the job opportunities in Laganside. An example of this is the Gasworks Employment Matching Service (GEMS) which aims to recruit 600 people to the project, placing half this group back into employment and providing the other half with the necessary education or training to enhance their long-term job prospects.

In order to develop a greater social mix in the area, the Laganside Corporation has been working with a number of agencies to provide housing for low-income groups in this area. For example, at May's Meadow, 48 housing units have been provided by Belfast Improved Housing for tenants who qualify for housing benefit.

In order to show support for local communities, Laganside Corporation offers grants of £250 for community groups and individuals to stage events within the Laganside area.

Check this!...

1 Why do local people believe their communities are dying out?

2 Describe two ways in which the Laganside Corporation is supporting local communities.

Key words to know

Waste management

3 Sustainable cities require management of traffic and waste problems

Increased levels of traffic congestion and waste are causing major problems for urban areas across the world. These problems need to be managed if cities are to have the ability to service the needs of future generations.

Case Study Extra

Waste management in Belfast

Back to...

The New Wider World **p185** for information on sustainable development in MEDCs.

Belfast City Council has joined with ten councils from the eastern region of Northern Ireland to form a partnership to provide an overarching waste management plan for the region. This grouping is called ARC21 to symbolise the group's co-ordinated sustainable approach to waste management in the twenty-first century.

The current trend of burying the vast majority of our waste products in landfill sites is unsustainable. The reasons for this include:

- the squandering of our natural resources, many of which are finite
- the high costs of removing and disposing of the waste
- the environmental problems caused by the disposal of waste in large holes called landfill sites
- the lack of suitable sites available for landfill.

The amount of household waste collected in Belfast increased during the 1990s but some reduction had occurred by 2002 (Figure 18.9).

Year	Total household waste
1996	132 199
1998	138 195
2000	144 851
2002	139 967

Figure 18.9 Quantities of household waste (in tonnes) for Belfast

Figure 18.10 shows where the household waste collected in Belfast goes to.

Reducing waste in Belfast

A large publicity drive across Northern Ireland has been encouraging people to 'wake up to waste' and practise 'the three R's':

- **Reduce**: not producing waste in the first place is the obvious solution. We can all play a part by thinking about how and why we produce waste.
- **Re-use**: many of the things we currently throw away could be re-used again and again with just a little thought and imagination, e.g. plastic bags.

Composted 1.7%
Recycled 2.3%
Landfill 96%

Belfast City Council

Figure 18.10 Destination of waste (2002)

● **Recycle**: waste products can be used to make new products, e.g. metal cans. This helps to conserve natural resources and energy.

Councils in Northern Ireland have been set a target of recovering 40 per cent of household waste by 2010 through recycling or composting. To meet this target, Belfast City Council has created a number of new services to help the public reduce the amount of waste going to landfill:

● Blue bins to collect paper for recycling have been provided for every household in the city.
● 'Kerbie' boxes have been introduced for inner city areas where there may be insufficient room for two bins per

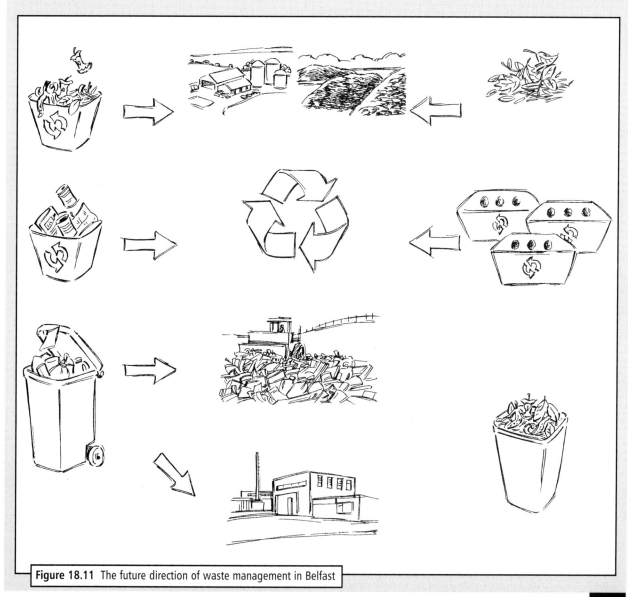

Figure 18.11 The future direction of waste management in Belfast

household. Plastics, textiles, glass and cans can be placed in these boxes.

- Thirty mini-bring sites have been established in residential areas for glass collection.
- Forty litter recycling bins have been placed around the city which enable the public to deposit paper, plastic bottles and metal cans for recycling.

Looking to the future

The Dargan Road landfill site, which takes Belfast's waste, will close in 2006. Landfill is not a sustainable solution to waste management, so local councils are exploring alternatives to reduce the need for more landfill sites.

Figure 18.11 shows a possible route to sustainable waste management for Belfast. Landfill could be replaced by waste incineration by 2010. The energy produced by this process could contribute to the generation of electricity.

Using your case study

This case study illustrates how waste management can contribute to the creation of sustainable urban environments.

Update

Go the *The NWW Coursemates* website for a link to the Belfast City web page for the latest news on waste management issues in Belfast.

Learn it!

1 List some examples of waste that could be re-used or recycled.

2 Describe two initiatives taken by Belfast City Council to reduce the amount of waste going to landfill.

3 Explain why landfill sites are not a sustainable solution to waste management.

Transport in urban areas

Traffic in general and the car in particular create numerous problems in urban areas. Most families in the more developed countries of Western Europe, North America and Japan own their own car. The car gives individual families greater mobility and, because it allows them to travel 'from door to door', gives them greater freedom of movement and choice in where they live, work, shop, are educated and find their recreation. However, it is the widespread use of the car that is bringing traffic in many large cities to a standstill and which is a major cause of urban environmental, economic and social problems. Everybody agrees that traffic problems in urban areas need drastic solutions, but people are less likely to agree on what those solutions might be.

Case Study Extra

Traffic control solutions in Athens

Back to...

The New Wider World **p67** Figure 4.23 for details of the impacts of traffic on urban areas.

The problem of air pollution in Athens was first noticed during the summertime in the 1970s when a yellowish-brown cloud was observed over the city. Athenians refer to the pollution as the *nefos* (literally meaning cloud). The nefos has been linked to a range of health problems – one

study suggested it caused more than 100 premature deaths a year. The famous landmarks of Athens, including the Acropolis, have also been affected by increased levels of chemical weathering.

Sources of pollution

Road traffic is the primary source of pollutants, with domestic heating systems and industries adding to the problem. In 1961 there were 39 000 vehicles on the roads of Athens but by 2004 the figure had risen to 1.4 million. There has been a corresponding fall in the numbers using public transport – from 70 per cent of Athenians in 1979 to 35 per cent in 2004.

Tackling the problem

In 1982 access to the city centre was restricted to registration plates ending in an odd number on odd dates, and plates ending in even numbers on even dates. Athenians bought second cars to get around the ban and as a result the problem increased, especially as these second cars were older and more polluting.

The scheme was modified in 1983 so that cars with plates ending in 0–4 and 5–9 were allowed access on alternate days. However, the reduction in the number of private cars was matched by an increase in the number of taxis.

In 1993 the EU passed a law that all cars sold in the EU must be fitted with a catalytic converter. Annual emissions tests in Athens from 1995 helped to improve air quality in the city during the 1990s (Figure 18.12) but efforts by the city authorities to tackle the nefos were given even greater urgency when the city was awarded the honour of hosting the 2004 Olympic Games.

A new tram system (Figure 18.13), which is expected to carry 35 000 passengers a day over 24 km of track, was built in time for the Games. It is hoped that the tram system, along with the metro which serves 470 000 people a day, will help reduce pollution from commuter traffic.

Pollution	Average contents 1987–93 (mg/m³)	Average contents 1994–2000 (mg/m³)	Reduction (%)	
Carbon monoxide	6.8	5.2	–23.5	**Figure 18.12** Pollution levels
Nitrogen oxides	187	138	–26.2	
Sulphur dioxide	74	39	–47.3	

Figure 18.13 One of 35 new trams in Athens created by Ferrari designer Pininfarina

Using your case study

Use this case study to answer questions on solutions to traffic problems in a city.

Case study links

Traffic congestion is a problem associated with urbanisation – covered in Chapter 17 pages 114–115.

Learn it!

1 What is the nefos?

2 What has caused the nefos?

3 Describe two schemes that have attempted to reduce the traffic problems in Athens.

EXAM PRACTICE

1 Urban redevelopment schemes attempt to improve the quality of the urban environment For a named case study, describe two ways in which this has been achieved. (4 marks)

2 State the meaning of the term *gentrification*. (2 marks)

3 Explain why the recycling of waste is necessary to create sustainable urban environments. (3 marks)

4 Using your case study of an EU city (excluding any in the UK), describe fully two measures taken to reduce the problems associated with traffic congestion. (4 marks)

EXAM TIPS

Read the questions carefully! In question 4 make specific reference, as directed, to an EU city that is not in the UK. Using a UK example, e.g. Manchester trams, will reduce your mark.

Back to ...

The NWW Coursemates website to check your answers to the exam practice question.

19 Skills

1 Map skills.

2 Interpreting photographs and observing landscapes.

3 Graphical skills.

4 Looking for patterns.

1 Map skills

Map scales

All maps should include a scale. This shows how distance on the map (in cm or mm) relates to real-life distance on the ground.

On a map, scale is shown in two ways (see Figure 19.1). Whenever you use a map you should try to use the scale to get an idea of the real-life distance between places.

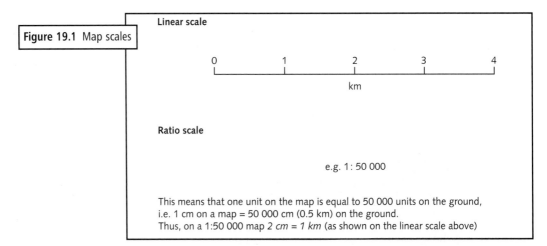

Figure 19.1 Map scales

Linear scale

0   1   2   3   4

km

Ratio scale

e.g. 1 : 50 000

This means that one unit on the map is equal to 50 000 units on the ground, i.e. 1 cm on a map = 50 000 cm (0.5 km) on the ground.
Thus, on a 1:50 000 map *2 cm = 1 km* (as shown on the linear scale above)

Back to ...

The New Wider World **pp41, 292 and 320** for examples of 1:50 000 OS maps.

There are many different scales of map. The larger the scale (e.g. 1:10 000), the more detail is shown; the smaller the scale (e.g. 1:1 000 000), the less detail is shown. Large-scale maps can show road layouts in towns, individual buildings and fields. Small-scale maps, like country maps in atlases, cover huge areas but give very little fine detail.

At GCSE level you are required to be able to read and interpret Ordnance Survey (OS) maps at the 1:50 000 (2 cm = 1 km) scale.

Back to ...

The New Wider World **inside back cover** to see a copy of the 1:50 000 OS map key.

Ordnance Survey map symbols

Maps contain a huge amount of information. This is made possible by using symbols instead of written labels, which would take up far too much space. Many symbols are clear in their meaning but they are always explained in a key. The key is usually found at the base or to the side of a map.

Key words to know

Eastings
Northings
Four-figure grid reference
Six-figure grid reference

Finding grid references

Ordnance Survey (OS) maps have gridlines drawn on them to enable locations to be given. The lines that run 'up and down' and increase in value from left to right (west to east), are called **eastings**. Those that run across the map and increase in value from bottom to top (south to north), are called **northings**.

To locate a grid square on a map, we use a **four-figure grid reference**. The first two digits refer to the easting value and the second two digits to the northing value.

To locate a point rather than a grid square, each grid square is split into 'tenths' to give a **six-figure grid reference**.

When giving a grid reference it is perfectly reasonable to estimate the 'tenths' but you can always use a ruler to be more precise. Exam mark schemes often allow one-tenth either side.

Giving compass directions

Figure 19.2 shows the compass directions. Usually on a map the direction north is 'straight up', but it is very important that you check the key when examining maps and diagrams. This is why it is also good practice to include a north point on all maps and diagrams that you

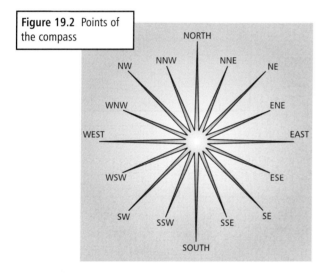

Figure 19.2 Points of the compass

Measuring distances

Every map should have a scale, usually in the form of a measured line (called a *linear scale*) with distances written alongside. To calculate a straight-line distance, you simply measure the distance on the map between the two points in question, using a ruler or the straight edge of a piece of paper. You then line up your ruler or paper alongside the linear scale to discover the actual distance on the ground in kilometres or miles.

A curved distance takes rather longer to work out. The best technique is to use the straight edge of a piece of paper to mark off sections of the curved line, effectively converting the curved distance into a straight-line distance. Look at Figure 19.3 to see how this technique works.

Remember to always give the units, for example kilometres, when writing your answer.

Back to ...

The New Wider World **p41** Figure 3.18: find the village of Thorngumbald. Most of the village is in grid square 2026.

The New Wider World **p41** Figure 3.18: locate the Post Office (P) in the village of Thorngumbald. Its six-figure grid reference is 208266. Notice how the eastings value is represented by the three digits 208 and the northings value is represented by the digits 266. It is the third digit of each set that is the 'tenths' value. Thus, the eastings value is 20 and 8/10ths and the northings value is 26 and 6/10ths.

The New Wider World **p41** Figure 3.18. When answering an exam question, be sure to express a compass direction carefully and precisely. For example, on this OS map Thorngumbald is to the south-east of Hedon, and Hedon is to the east of Salt End.

Figure 19.3 Measuring a curved distance

1. Place the straight edge of the paper alongside the route. Mark on the start (S). Look along the edge of the paper and mark off the point where the curved line no longer runs alongside the paper.

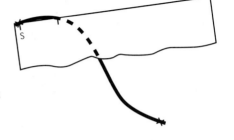

2. Carefully pivot the paper at this point until the curved line once again runs alongside. Continue along the curved line marking off the straight segments until you reach the finish. Mark this on the paper (F).

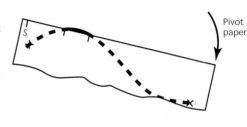

3. Measure the total straight-line distance using a ruler and convert to kilometres using the linear scale on the map.

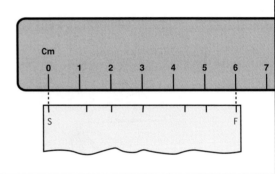

Key word to know

Sketch map

Drawing sketch maps

A **sketch map** is a simplified map that is not drawn absolutely to scale. However, it is important to add a scale even if it is just an approximation.

A sketch map is very useful because the person drawing it can decide what to include and what to leave out. It may be that only information about the physical landscape is needed or, alternatively, just the settlements and roads.

A sketch map can be drawn from any kind of map, including OS maps, maps taken from atlases, or those based on maps seen on the internet.

To draw a sketch map you should follow these steps:

- Start by drawing a frame. Make sure that the shape of the frame matches the shape of the area on the original map. It might be a square or a rectangle. Make your frame bigger or smaller than the original if you want to enlarge or reduce it.
- Now carefully transfer the information that you require from the original map onto your sketch map. You could use grid lines to help you – this is easy if your original map is an OS map – or simply draw one or two major guiding features, such as roads or rivers.
- Once complete, you can use colour and shading if you wish, although black-and-white sketches are often the most successful.

128

- Label and annotate as required (see below), and don't forget to include an approximate scale, a north point and a title.

Labels and annotations

- **Labels** are often single words identifying, for example, physical features or names of places.
- **Annotations** are usually short sentences giving a description or explanation. They are more detailed and often more useful than labels.

Remember that most of the credit for a sketch map will relate to your labels and annotations, which show your ability to interpret the map.

Key words to know

Labels
Annotations

Drawing a cross-section

A **cross-section** is an imaginary slice through a landscape. It is very useful because it helps you to visualise what a landscape actually looks like.

To draw a cross-section you need a piece of scrap paper, a sharp pencil, a ruler and an eraser. The stages of construction are shown in Figure 19.4.

Key words to know

Cross-section

Figure 19.4 Drawing a cross-section

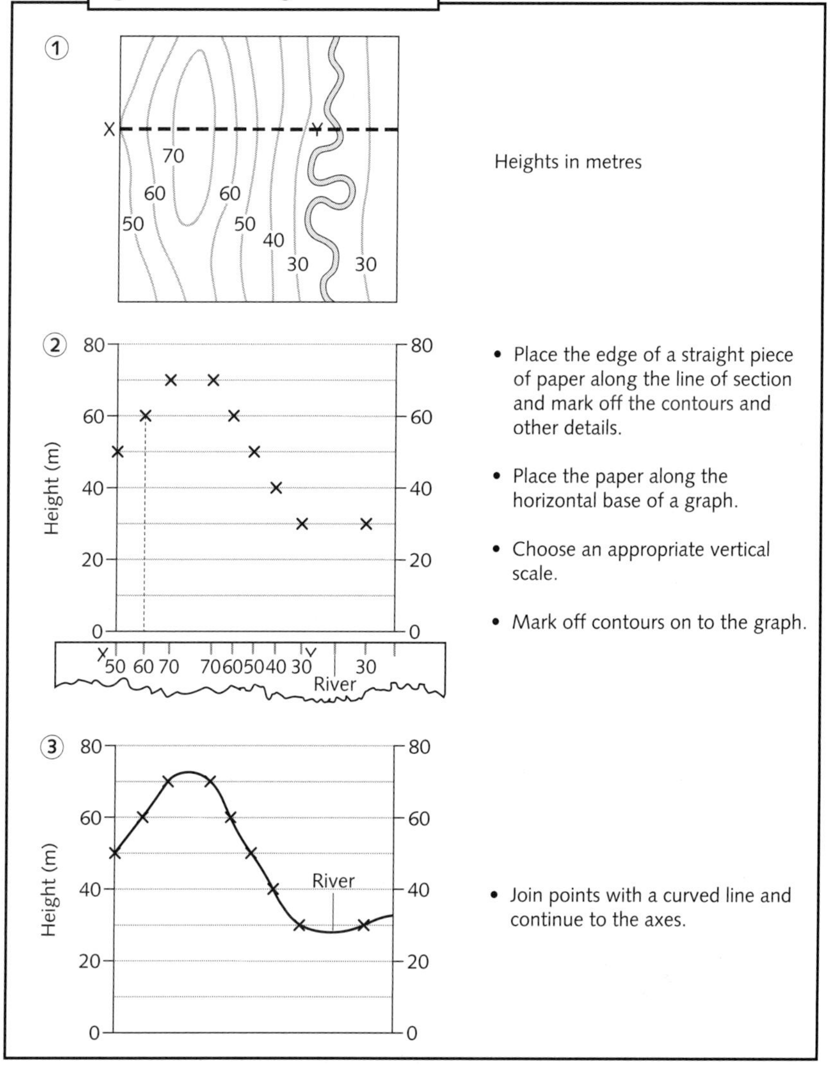

1
X
Y
70
60
60
50
50
40
30
30
Heights in metres
2
Height (m)
80
60
40
20
0
50 60 70 70605040 30 30
River
• Place the edge of a straight piece of paper along the line of section and mark off the contours and other details.
• Place the paper along the horizontal base of a graph.
• Choose an appropriate vertical scale.
• Mark off contours on to the graph.
3
River
• Join points with a curved line and continue to the axes.

As you complete your cross-section, bear in mind the following points:

- Double-check that you have written down the correct height values.
- Make your vertical scale as realistic as possible – don't exaggerate it so much that you create a totally unreal landscape.
- Complete the cross-section to both vertical axes by carrying on the trend of the landscape.
- Label any features.
- Complete axes labels and give grid references for each end of your cross-section.
- Give your cross-section a title.

A *long profile* is very similar to a cross-section, although it usually involves marking off contour values along a curved distance (see 'Measuring distances' on pages 127–128). Long profiles are most commonly drawn to show changes down a river valley.

Describing the physical landscape

Key words to know

Relief
Drainage

At GCSE level you are required to explore the ways that relief is presented on OS maps and to identify major relief features.

Relief is the geographical term used to describe the lie of the land. To gain the most marks in an exam you should comment on:

- The height of the land, using actual figures taken from contours or spot heights to support your points. Using words like 'high' and 'low' is fairly meaningless, without the use of actual figures. Refer to different areas or parts of the map using compass directions to enable you to be precise.
- The slope of the land – is the land flat, or sloping? Which way do the slopes face? Are the slopes gentle or steep? Are there bare cliffs exposed? Again, it is important to give precise supporting information such as grid references, compass directions, etc.
- The presence of features such as valleys, dry valleys, escarpments, etc. Refer to names and use grid references.

Describing the human landscape

Ordnance Survey maps contain a lot of information about aspects of human geography, for example roads, settlements, functions and industry.

Back to ...

The New Wider World **p41**
Figure 3.18: study the roads, settlements, functions and industry.

- **Roads** Different colours are used to show the various types of road. When describing road networks, refer to the type of road and use road numbers whenever possible. For example, the main road passing through Thorngumbald (2026) is the A1033. Use compass directions when describing the pattern of roads. Look out for roads that might be intended to act as by-passes, such as the A1033 to the south of Hedon. Road networks are clearly visible in settlements and it is possible to identify patterns. Notice how in grid square 1430 the roads tend to form a regular grid pattern, suggesting that they are probably part of an older terraced housing area. A more modern housing area, with curved roads and cul-de-sacs, can be found in grid square 1432.

- **Settlements** The pale pink/brown colour on the map shows the extent of the built-up areas. This is where the houses and shops are. The white spaces in between are areas of open ground, such as parks. Some important buildings such as schools – you can see several of these on the outskirts of Hull – are shown separately. The shapes of settlements (for example, whether they are nucleated or linear) can be readily identified.
- **Functions** There are several functions and services shown on the map. In Preston just to the north of Hedon, there is a Post Office, a public house, several places of worship, a school and a sports centre. The number and type of functions can be used to suggest a settlement hierarchy, though it is important to remember that not all functions, particularly shops, are shown on OS maps.
- **Industry** Industrial buildings are usually large and are often arranged in a regular pattern. A good example is the Works to the south of Salt End in grid squares 1627 and 1628. Notice how, in common with many industrial sites, this is on the outskirts of the main town where there is plenty of relatively cheap land available. It has easy access to main roads and, in this case, has a jetty into the river. You can see other industrial buildings alongside the A1033 to the west of Salt End.

Describing patterns on specialist maps

In addition to OS maps, there are many specialist maps, e.g. geological maps, weather maps, etc.
- Geological maps show the different types of rock below the ground surface.
- Soil maps show different types of soil.
- Weather maps (synoptic charts) show weather information.

To interpret specialist maps you should make good use of the key, which will tell you the meaning of the symbols. In describing what the maps show, apply all the principles of good practice described above. Refer to specific locations, give facts and figures, refer to distances and compass directions, etc. You may be asked to relate a specialist map to an OS map.

2 Interpreting photographs and observing landscapes

Interpreting ground photographs

Ground photographs are photographs taken by someone standing on the ground. They show what a place looks like as we would see it if we were standing on the ground.

To interpret a ground photograph you need to look at it closely and look for clues to help you understand what is happening. For example, if trees are in leaf and people are wearing shorts then it was probably taken in the summer.

Back to …

Figure 6.1 on p38 which shows the geology of Cuilcagh Mountain in County Fermanagh.

The New Wider World **pp205–206** Figures 12.13, 12.15 and 12.16 which are all examples of weather maps.

The New Wider World **p150** Figures 9.33–9.34, which show some features of recycling and appropriate technology in LEDCs. In an exam, you could be asked to describe in detail what the people are doing.

Back to ...

The New Wider World **p88**
Figure 5.26, which is an
oblique aerial photograph
of the new town
Barra di Tijuca near
Rio de Janeiro in Brazil. It shows
the layout of the settlement,
with the shopping malls and car
parks in the foreground, the
high-rise apartments in the right
background and the mountains
in the far distance.

Back to ...

The New Wider World **p205**
Figure 12.12 for a satellite image
of a passing depression.

Key words to know

Sketch

Interpreting aerial photographs

Aerial photographs give us much the same view of an area as we would see when looking out of an aeroplane window. Vertical aerial photographs look directly down on an area much as a map does. Oblique aerial photographs look down at an area at an angle.

Aerial photographs are excellent in showing what an area looks like. They can help us understand and bring to life the detail shown on a map.

You may well be required to relate an aerial photograph to a map extract. Usually you will be asked to work out which way the photograph is looking. To do this, you first need to locate on the map extract some of the features shown at the bottom, middle and top of the photograph. This gives you a line of sight. Then use the compass directions on the map to help you work out which way the photograph is looking.

Interpreting satellite photographs and images

Satellites can provide us with very accurate and detailed photographs often covering large areas of the Earth's surface. Many modern maps are produced using satellite photographs because they are so accurate and up to date.

Computers can create satellite images that use false colours to help identify features of interest, for example green crops, surface water or settlements.

Drawing a sketch from a photograph

It is important to realise that the purpose of a **sketch** is to identify the main geographical characteristics of the landscape. It is not necessary to produce a brilliant artistic drawing; clarity and accuracy are all that is needed. The majority of marks awarded in an exam are given for accurate labels and annotations.

To draw a sketch, you first need to draw a frame to the same general shape of the photograph. Then draw one or two major lines that will subsequently act as guidelines for the rest of your sketch. You could draw the profile of a slope or a hilltop, or a road or river, for example. Consider what it is that you are trying to show and concentrate on these aspects; it may be river features or the pattern of settlements. Don't take time drawing a lot of detail that is not required and only serves to confuse.

Always use a good sharp pencil and don't be afraid to rub things out as you go along.

Finally, remember to label or annotate (detailed labels) your sketch to identify the features, and give your sketch a title.

Figure 19.6 is an annotated sketch map based on the photograph of a meander on the Sruh Croppa River in County Fermanagh (Figure 19.5).

Figure 19.5 A meander on the Sruh Croppa River, County Fermanagh

Slip-off slope (deposition)

Rock deposited in river

River cliff (erosion)

undercutting of river bank

Figure 19.6 An annotated sketch of the meander on the Sruh Croppa River shown in Figure 19.5

Drawing field sketches

A **field sketch** is a sketch drawn outside (in the field) to show a particular view. Field sketches are often used to show aspects of the physical landscape, for example a waterfall or cliff. However, they can also be used to show features of the human landscape, for example aspects of village architecture or farming land use.

To draw a field sketch, you should follow the guidelines in 'Drawing a sketch from a photograph' on pages 132–133. Decide how large an area you wish to sketch and draw a frame to the appropriate size and shape. Take time to represent the landscape accurately within your frame but avoid the temptation to strive for a work of art! It is the labels and annotations that are most valuable.

3 Graphical skills

Drawing line graphs

A **line graph** shows continuous changes over a period of time, for example stream flow or population change. It is a very common and effective technique to use, but it is important to remember that time, which is shown on the horizontal axis, must have an equal spacing, for example from year to year.

Drawing bar graphs and histograms

Bar graphs and histograms are one of the most common methods used to display statistical information. However, they are not exactly the same.

- A **bar graph** or chart is used to show the frequency or amount of a number of different categories, such as types of goods bought from a supermarket. The bars are drawn with a gap between them and they are coloured or shaded differently because they are unconnected (see Figure 19.7).

Key word to know

Field sketch

Key words to know

Line graph
Bar graph
Histogram
Pie chart
Triangular graph
Rose diagram
Proportional circle
Scattergraph
Best-fit line

Back to ...

The New Wider World **p10** Figure 1.10, which is a line graph showing the growth in world population since 1800. Notice that the points have been joined up with a freehand curve, which is usually the case with such graphs.

Back to ...

The New Wider World **p164**
Figure 10.15, which is a rainfall climate graph and is an example of a histogram. The monthly rainfall values form part of the total annual rainfall, so they can be drawn as 'touching' bars.

The New Wider World **p14**
Figure 1.17 which is a composite bar chart showing the differences between male and female life expectancy in selected countries.

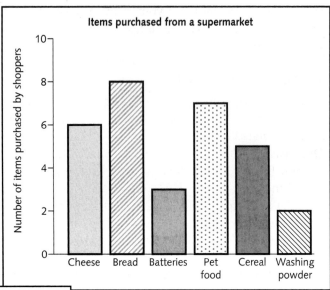

Figure 19.7 A bar graph

- A **histogram** also uses blocks but with no gaps between them. This is because a histogram is drawn when there is continuous data (such as daily rainfall values over a period of a month) or the values are all part of a single survey, for example the sizes of particles in a sediment sample. As the bars are effectively connected, a single colour or type of shading is used.

It is possible to use multiple bar charts and 'split' or composite bar charts to show two or more pieces of information at the same time.

Drawing pie charts

A **pie chart** is quite simply a circle divided into segments, rather like slicing a cake! It is usually drawn to show the proportions of a total, for example the number of shoppers visiting a supermarket each day during one week. Pie charts work best when they have between 4 and 10 segments; pie charts with only one segment are a waste of time and those with many segments become too confusing.

When drawing a pie chart, remember to convert your values into degrees (for percentages multiply by 3.6).

Back to ...

The New Wider World **p173**
Figure 10.36 which uses pie charts to show statistics for the Lake District National Park.

The New Wider World **p186**
Figure 11.11 which compares types of trade for a number of different countries.

The New Wider World **p93**
Figure 6.4 which shows how employment structure data can be displayed on a triangular graph.

Drawing triangular graphs

A **triangular graph** enables three values to be plotted at the same time to produce a single point. The values take the form of percentages that add up to 100. They are commonly used to show soil texture, employment and types of mass movement.

Drawing rose diagrams

A **rose diagram** shows the orientation of observed data, for example wind direction (Figure 19.8). Bars are drawn from an octagonal central shape to represent the number or frequency of each direction.

Drawing proportional symbols

Proportional circles are a very effective way to show data, particularly on a base map where spatial variations can be seen. However, they are rather tricky to draw and you will need to choose your scale carefully.

Figure 19.8 A wind rose for a UK weather station

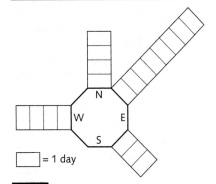

☐ = 1 day

Select a scale for the radius of your circle. As it is the *area* of the circle that needs to be proportional, you must use the square root value as your radius distance.

Drawing scattergraphs

If you think that two sets of data are related, then the information can be plotted on a graph called a **scattergraph**. To complete a scattergraph you should do the following:

- Draw two graph axes in the normal way, but try to put the variable that is thought to be causing the change in the other (called the *independent variable*) on the horizontal (*x*) axis. In Figure 19.9, the wealth of a country (GNP) is thought to be responsible for the number of doctors.
- Use each pair of values to plot a single point on the graph using a cross.
- Use a **best-fit line** to clarify the trend of the points if there is one (see Figure 19.9). Your best-fit line should pass roughly through the centre of the points so that there is approximately the same number of points on either side of the line. Use a ruler to draw a straight line. The best-fit line does *not* need to pass through the origin. The resultant pattern can now be described.

Drawing flow lines

Flow lines are an excellent way to show movement, for example where people visiting a particular country have come from. Each line is drawn with its width proportional to its value, for example 1 cm = 10 million tourists. Flow lines are most effective when drawn on a base map.

Drawing choropleth maps

A **choropleth map** is a map that uses different colours or density of shading to show the distribution of data categories.

Notice the following key features in Figure 1.2 on p5 of *The New Wider World*:

- The base map shows regions or areas, in this case countries.
- Data is divided into a number of groups or categories. Ideally there should be between four and six categories. Notice that the category values do not overlap.
- The darker the shading, the higher the value.
- The map has a powerful and immediate visual impact; it is an effective form of mapping.

Drawing isopleth maps

An **isopleth map** is a map that uses lines of equal value to show patterns. Contours are a good example of isopleths, and are usually drawn at intervals of 10 metres.

Some of the most common isopleth maps are drawn to show aspects of weather and climate, e.g. isobars show pressure, and isotherms show temperature.

Whilst isopleth maps are rather difficult maps to draw, they are very effective at showing patterns, particularly when they are superimposed on a base map.

To draw an isopleth map, you need to mark your observed data onto a base map or sheet of tracing paper/acetate. You then need to consider

Back to ...

The New Wider World **p93** Figure 6.3: proportional circles are used very effectively to show regional variations in employment structures in the UK. Notice how the circles are also used as pie charts to show the different types of employment. This complex method of data presentation will score highly in any coursework that you undertake.

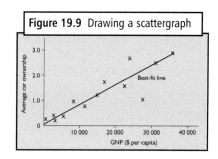

Figure 19.9 Drawing a scattergraph

Key words to know

Flow lines
Choropleth map
Isopleth map
Topological map

Back to ...

The New Wider World **p178** question 4 which includes a flow map showing the numbers of tourists travelling to Spain. Notice that the largest number of tourists come from France.

The New Wider World **p201** Figures 12.3 and 12.4, in which the isotherms have been drawn at 1° intervals.

Back to ...

The New Wider World **p4**
Figure 1.1: a description of the distribution of world population as shown here might be as follows:

'World population is unevenly distributed. In some parts of the world, for example north-west Europe, India, eastern China and south-east Africa, there is a dense population distribution. However, large parts of the world have a relatively low population density, for example Canada, much of the Russian Federation, north Africa and much of Australia.'

how many lines to attempt to draw and at what intervals you will draw them. This decision is largely 'trial and error' and you may need to have a go in rough first.

Look at Figure 19.10 to see how isopleths are drawn. Notice how they pass between values that are higher and lower than the value of the line. Just remember that all values to one side of a line will be higher, and all those to the other side will be lower.

There is a degree of individual determination and decision-making, so do not worry if your map turns out to be slightly different from those of your neighbours.

Drawing topological maps

A **topological map** is a map that is not drawn to a true distance scale. Whilst it shows where places are relative to each other, it often appears distorted.

Figure 19.11 is a topological map which shows the railway network of Northern Ireland. Whilst stations are located correctly according to their position on the various lines, no attempt has been made to draw the map to a true distance scale.

Topological maps can be very effective and can stimulate discussion, such as those drawn to a scale of time taken rather than distance.

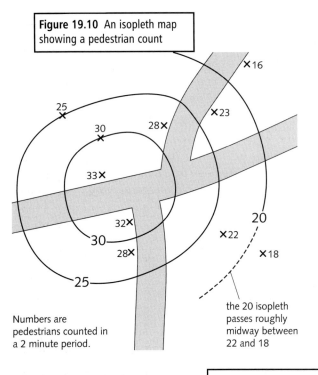

Figure 19.10 An isopleth map showing a pedestrian count

Numbers are pedestrians counted in a 2 minute period.

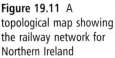

the 20 isopleth passes roughly midway between 22 and 18

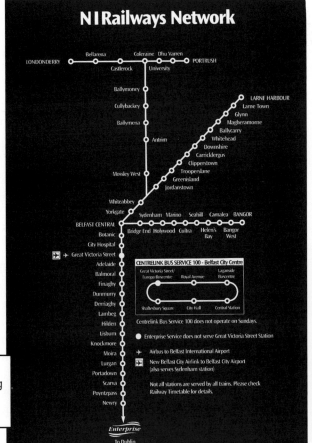

Figure 19.11 A topological map showing the railway network for Northern Ireland

4 Looking for patterns

How to 'describe'

To **describe** a map, photograph or diagram you need to put into words what it shows. Start by describing the overall picture or pattern. Refer to the information available on the map, photograph or diagram and give actual facts and figures to support your statements. Then, if appropriate, look for any exceptions (called *anomalies*) to the general pattern. The most important thing is to be as precise and detailed as you can. Also, avoid giving reasons unless you are specifically asked to 'explain'.

How to 'compare' and 'contrast'

To **compare** or **contrast**, you need to write about similarities and differences, for example between two areas on a map. It is essential to make comparisons all the way through your answer, so you should use words like 'whereas' or 'compared with'. Avoid the temptation to write separate paragraphs on the two areas under discussion.

As with making a description, you should refer to places and data wherever possible.

How to 'explain' or 'give reasons'

To **explain** patterns on maps or diagrams you need to try to think of reasons why they exist. This is much more difficult and will test your understanding of geography. You may need to refer to other maps and diagrams to help you. For example, to explain the hydrographs in Figure 17.6 on p280 of *The New Wider World* you could write:

'The main reason why the hydrograph for drainage basin A has a higher peak and more rapidly rising and falling limbs than the hydrograph for drainage basin B is because there is a much higher drainage density in basin A than in B. In basin A, water passes quickly into river channels and then it flows rapidly to the gauging station resulting in a dramatic hydrograph. In basin B, the lower drainage density means that it takes far longer for water to pass through the system hence the longer time lag and the flatter hydrograph.'

You will often be awarded marks for suggesting a reasonable explanation even if it is not absolutely accurate; an examiner will give you credit for making a reasonable suggestion.

How to 'analyse'

An **analysis** is very similar to an explanation except that it usually involves more detail and a much greater use of facts and figures. When conducting your coursework you will probably be required to **analyse** your data.

Key words to know

Describe
Compare and contrast

Back to ...

The New Wider World **pp268–269** Figures 16.20 and 16.22: a comparison between the two volcanic eruptions shown in these photographs might read as follows:

'In Figure 16.20 the volcano is erupting large quantities of red-hot lava, whereas the volcano in Figure 16.22 is erupting dense black clouds of ash and pyroclastics. An ash cloud is rising into the atmosphere from the volcano in Figure 16.22, whereas there is no ash cloud in Figure 16.20. Both eruptions look very dramatic and dangerous.'

Key words to know

Explain
Analyse

Back to ...

The New Wider World **p81** Figure 17.8: an analysis of this complex hydrograph is given in the Case Study box. Notice that it involves a detailed study of the graph together with an interpretation of the effects of drainage basin characteristics on river flow.